TELEVISED LEGISLATURES: POLITICAL INFORMATION TECHNOLOGY AND PUBLIC CHOICE

TELEVISED LEGISLATURES: POLITICAL INFORMATION TECHNOLOGY AND PUBLIC CHOICE

W. Mark Crain
Center for Study of Public Choice
George Mason University
Fairfax, Virginia 22030

Brian L. Goff
Economics Department
Western Kentucky University
Bowling Green, Kentucky 42101

Kluwer Academic Publishers
Boston/Dordrecht/Lancaster

Distributors for North America:
Kluwer Academic Publishers
101 Philip Drive
Assinippi Park
Norwell, Massachusetts 02061, USA

Distributors for the UK and Ireland:
Kluwer Academic Publishers
MTP Press Limited
Falcon House, Queen Square
Lancaster LA1 1RN, UNITED KINGDOM

Distributors for all other countries:
Kluwer Academic Publishers Group
Distribution Centre
Post Office Box 322
3300 AH Dordrecht, THE NETHERLANDS

Library of Congress Cataloging-in-Publication Data

Crain, W. Mark.
    Televised legislatures : political information, technology, and
public choice / authors, W. Mark Crain, Brian L. Goff.
        p. cm.
    Bibliography: p.
    Includes index.
    ISBN 0-89838-262-9 (U.S.)
    1. United States. Congress—Television broadcasting of
proceedings.   2. Legislative bodies—United States—States—
Television broadcasting of proceedings.   3. Voting—United States.
4. Social choice.   I. Goff, Brian L.   II. Title.
JK1129.C73   1988   87-35559
328.73—dc19   CIP

Printed in the United States of America

To RDT.

CONTENTS

TABLES AND FIGURES

List of Tables

List of Figures

PREFACE

Our interest in studying televised legislatures was kindled by two episodes. The first was a series of rejections by the U.S. Senate between 1984 and 1986 of resolutions to permit live television coverage of floor proceedings. The second was the 1984 "Camscam affair," the media label given to a partisan war over camera coverage of U.S. House proceedings. Each episode, if nothing else, made plain the intensity of the feelings that elected representatives feel about televised sessions. Legislative television was not taken lightly by those who had the most to gain or lose.

Surveys indicate that legislative watchers, "C-SPAN junkies," number in the millions and penetration of cable access to televised sessions numbered nearly 40 million in 1986. In addition to the direct viewers, television news programs increasingly use excerpts from the televised sessions as enhancements and sources for political reporting. Televising legislatures, in short, has attracted much new attention to the process of legislating. The innovation and diffusion of the electronic Acropolis has transformed politics in the U.S. Yet, its impact on the democratic process has attracted little notice except from a few political journalists.

Our predilections as economists working in the public choice tradition led us into the analysis of several questions surrounding television: What do televised sessions provide for legislators? How are incumbent reelection bids affected? Do all incumbents benefit? How are legislative sessions changed? Has the enactment of laws been influenced? For the most part, these questions had received only cursory treatment.

Our analysis of the impact of televised legislatures naturally leads us into a bigger picture involving more general issues about technological change, politics, and constitutional design. We will touch on these broader questions, as well as proposals for constitutional reform, in the pages that follow.

Acknowledgements

We express our appreciation for partial financial support to the Center for

Study of Public Choice and the Center for the Study of Market Processes. Several individuals have contributed time and effort to this project. A little bit of Bob Tollison can be found in every chapter. In addition, we thank Jim Buchanan, Kevin Grier, Bill Landes, Don Leavens, Jim Miller, Tom Reid, Bill Shughart, Scott Thomas, Gordon Tullock and Asghar Zardkoohi. John Lott has been particularly interested in the project and our thoughts are clearer due to his efforts. Finally, we are grateful to Libby Masaitis, Carol Robert, and Sarah Seeberg for their services and patience. We are responsible for all remaining errors.

TELEVISED LEGISLATURES: POLITICAL INFORMATION TECHNOLOGY AND PUBLIC CHOICE

Chapter 1

THE ARCHITECTURE OF CONSTITUTIONS

Politics in America can be improved is the optimistic side to this book. The other side is that the Constitution may be too difficult to change in order to respond to the pressures that have come with 200 years. The U.S. political structure is stressed because the style of the Constitution suits the state of communications in the time of its designers.

The Founding Fathers favored constitutional rules that economized on the costs of democratic decision-making. In their time the costs of an informed citizenry and political participation were formidable. If political decisions were costless, we might not opt for representative democracy over direct democracy. After all, not everyone is a legislator because there is more to life than political discourse and voting.

Changes in the feasibility of sending and receiving political information have fundamentally changed the relationship between citizens and elected representatives. This change, in turn, has spurred many adjustments that we will trace throughout national and state politics in the U.S. We limit ourselves in this book to the study of the forces of technological change on the democratic system. Telecommunications and its impact on the performance of the American political process is the specific subject to be analyzed. Yet, even this aspect of politics is far too broad for one study, if the study is to go into analytical depth. We will close the lens of our analysis tighter and focus on a very small segment of technological innovations, namely, the innovation of televising legislatures. We will examine, for example, how live legislative television has changed voter behavior in national and state elections.

The ancient Greeks contended that democracy would not survive once there were too many citizens to fit on the Acropolis. The ability of the governed to listen to their leader speak was thought to be critical for their political system. The way that citizens learn about and keep track of their legislators is a pivotal issue in the performance of democratic government. The Founding Fathers had this issue firmly in mind as they designed the architecture of the United States Constitution. The function they valued most was control of political power, and this function depended on an informed citizenry. As with the ancient Greeks, the Founding Fathers recognized that democratic institutions are related to society's ability to communicate.

Television is the electronic Acropolis. It has enlarged the audience that can observe and listen to legislators at work. What comes with the expanded audience of the electronic Acropolis are new opportunities for control. Unfortunately, not all of the opportunities are positive from the standpoint of protecting individual liberty. New telecommunications technologies also create new opportunities for manipulation and political abuse.

In any case, we have no interest in rolling back the clock on technology. We seek to uncover lessons about the impact of technology on the democratic process that may guide our future thinking. With this in mind, our analysis is potentially useful, even though we rule out the idea of going back to the state of non-televised legislatures. Our intent is not to stuff technology back in the box.

The broader point is that technological innovations applied to politics, such as televising legislatures, can make existing "constitutional" rules obsolete and call for new ones. In short, solutions to problems generated by new technology in politics do not necessarily require resistance to change, but rather, understanding and adapting to change.

Institutions matter. To the follower of public choice theory, this two-word sentence is practically a motto. In this book we use public choice theory to examine institutions and the political effects of information technology. In an age where innovations in the technology of telecommunications are broad-ranging, our narrow interest in studying televised legislatures would hardly seem to raise an eyebrow. A part of the public choice tradition, however, is to squint and study society's institutions closely, even those that seem, on the surface, to be inconsequential. Measures of the impact of televising legislatures on the performance of American politics, the empirical objective of this book, are found through the public choice vision.

Public choice theorists usually begin with the working behavioral postulate of self-interest. This abstraction is simply that the politician, not unlike the businessman or consumer, takes self-interest into account in making decisions. It is natural for the public choice economist to question new institutions in terms of how the self-interests of individuals, or groups of individuals, are affected by them.

For example, how has televising legislatures affected the reelection prospects for incumbents? It is easy to understand why incumbents will be reluctant to adopt rules that make them more vulnerable. One of the specific questions that motivated this book is whether cameras in the legislative chambers are the equivalent of "free" advertising for incumbent candidates. Are the broadcasts, in effect, another incumbent protection device? We find that televised sessions do affect election outcomes, and that the specific effect is tied to the demographics of a representative's district. Some incumbents are helped, others are hurt and, thus, in concrete ways political influence is redistributed from some groups to others. There are additional effects of televising sessions on the process of lawmaking. For more examples, we examine the effects of live television coverage on the pace of legislative activity, on the amount of legislation produced, and on the nature of the legislation that gets enacted.

The analysis and evidence on how politics in the U.S. has been changed by information technology forms the basis for suggesting constitutional reforms. We advocate change towards longer electoral terms, for example. The changes we discuss can be made within the political philosophy of the existing constitutional architecture. Put differently, if the Founding Fathers were rewriting the Constitution 200 years later, but using their original principles, they would not reset particular variables to the same values. The architects of the U.S. Constitution held principles of design that were not meant to freeze it in time. Instead, their principles are general enough to leave many options open, such as the choice of a particular term length, or the size of a given legislature.

It is only a short hop in logic to expect the best rules for democratic government to be a function of the state of communications technology. The problems of this type that strain the political process do not arise out of a failure or breakdown in basic philosophy. Instead, they arise out of the simple recognition that information technology has dramatically changed the costs of operating the democratic process in the U.S. The process of democracy operates differently than it did 200 years ago when the Founding Fathers were filling in the planks for quite specific structural decisions. Innovations in telecommunications have caused changes in the behavior of voters and legislators. These changes have not made the political philosophy of the Founding Fathers obsolete. Rather, the changes have made obsolete the choices for some of the constitutional "variables," selected within their original architectural paradigm.

Our proposals for reform do not rely on a new theory of constitutions. To attempt to resolve the problems in the U.S. that are suggested by our study, much more modest adjustments may be all that are required. This mind-set towards reform suggests something further; the changes that have occurred in voter and legislator behavior leave more opportunities for the political system to perform better than were feasible in the age of the Constitution writers. We will return to the issue of constitutional reforms in the final chapter of the book.

Why and how has the electronic Acropolis changed the democratic process in the U.S.? What evidence is there that televising a legislature matters? Addressing these questions occupies the bulk of the pages that follow. In Chapter

2 we pick-up with the question of "why?". The literature on the economic theory of information provides a different and useful perspective on why televising legislatures has changed the process. In particular, the product advertising literature distinguishes types of advertising according to the ways that consumers obtain information about products. This distinction is central to the analysis of political information. The way that voters learn about politicians is a fairly exact analogy to the way consumers learn about products.

In the standard "goods" market, consumers use different techniques to economize on information costs. The best technique for a consumer to learn about products in the marketplace depends on the type of item that is going to be purchased. For example, is it an infrequently purchased item? In a nutshell (there is more in Chapter 2), this consumer pattern determines the nature of the advertising practice adopted by the product's producers. By analogy to politics, this will mean that legislators, like firms, will behave differently as citizens find more economical options to stay politically informed. Information technology is centrally important because, as it diffuses through the political system, the costs and feasibilities of staying informed are changed.

We take up the question of "how?" in Chapter 3. How has the electronic Acropolis changed U.S. politics? Voters, interest groups, and the media find it cheaper and more accurate to monitor legislator actions through televised sessions. More weight comes to be placed on specific political decisions of legislators, than on age-old factors like name recognition, political reputation, or party affiliation. When voters are shopping around at election time, they are informed differently about legislative candidates because qualities about incumbent legislators have been communicated via televised sessions. The broadcasts expose legislator traits to constituents that would be difficult for them to discover in other ways. Televised sessions lower the costs to voters of gathering political details, which affects voting decisions and, in turn, election outcomes. The exact impact of legislative television on election outcomes depends on constituent diversity. Summarizing the analysis in Chapter 3, incumbents from homogeneous constituencies are helped by television, and incumbents from heterogeneous constituencies are hurt.

The effects of televising legislatures on election outcomes in the U.S. are examined empirically in Chapters 4 and 5. In Chapter 4 we focus on election results for state legislatures, and in Chapter 5 we examine the effects on election results for the U.S. House of Representatives. Summarizing once again, we find empirical support for our theoretical analysis that the legislator–voter relationship has been changed by legislative television.

In Chapter 6 we analyze the impact of television on legislative proceedings and output. Live television coverage has altered the way that business is conducted and the amount of legislation that gets considered. We offer evidence of these effects using data on state legislatures. We compare the pace and volume of activity in states with versus those without television cameras covering their sessions. We find evidence that the legislative process adjusts to the cameras in systematic, predictable ways. In general, legislators who are made more vulnerable by broadcasts of the proceedings will produce more bills, and at a faster pace, in order to offset these ill effects. On the other hand, we discover that sessions tend to be more drawn out with less legislation passed, when legislators are helped electorally by televised coverage of the proceedings.

Chapter 7 investigates the politics of the legislative decision to implement live television. The reluctance of the U.S. Senate and the refusal of certain states to televise highlights the diversity of the effects across political jurisdictions. For example, the added exposure makes some legislators more vulnerable, and we would expect the strongest opposition to be voiced by this group. How televised sessions are likely to effect vote returns are used as a basis for predicting a legislator's support or opposition to television. From the theoretical framework and empirical evidence gathered in Chapters 2 through 6, we expect legislators from diverse districts to be less likely to favor televised sessions than legislators from monolithic districts. The evidence in Chapter 7 using U.S. Senate data supports this prediction.

In the final Chapter we summarize briefly and then get back into the mode of constitutional reform. We argue that the electronic Acropolis has changed fundamentally the function of elections in controlling political power. The function of reelection as a disciplinary device is less important to democratic performance than it was in times where the costs of gathering political information were much higher. To give one example, innovations in political information technology mean that elections can be held less frequently; that is, terms can be longer. We argue that adjustments of this type can be made without unleashing political power, which keeps us squarely within the architecture fancied by the Founding Fathers.

Chapter 2

POLITICAL INFORMATION TECHNOLOGY
AND PUBLIC CHOICE: BACKGROUND

Voter Shopping: Experience and Search

When voters vote, their choices are influenced by what they know about candidates. What is not known is similarly influential. What voters know and do not know depends on how much it costs to become informed politically. Individuals take into consideration the costs of political information in political transactions, just as in the market.

Information technology determines the relationship between inputs and outputs of information. This relationship influences what voters know because it dictates how they know it and how much it costs. The effects on the democratic process of the dynamics of technological innovation are what we want to describe. The way that voters become informed about political candidates is the specific part of the process on which we focus.

Innovations change the way voters become informed because when it is generally expensive for voters to keep track of legislators or to know where candidates stand on issues, the democratic process tends to rely on other institutions for monitoring and controlling politicians. Political parties serve this function in the U.S. and other countries. Parties offer affiliations that are brandnames which implicitly guarantee certain qualities of candidates who use their label. Likewise, an incumbent's reputation is an important consideration to voters when it is difficult to know much about his particular views. Consider the opposite extreme; one in which voters could know, costlessly, the way candidates felt about any issue. In such a world, party affiliations and incumbent reputations would be of less value to voters.

In this sense, technology determines the way voters choose to learn and the type of information they will have about candidates. The technology of political information is not static, and the dynamic of innovation is a force that changes the voter's choices. To develop the tie between technological innovation and voter behavior, we borrow directly from the analysis of product advertising. An emphasis is placed on analogies between the content of advertising for "everyday" products and the advertising of political services.

Various concepts, related to the theory of political information, and voter responses to information are introduced in the discussion below. The material we survey here provides a short background into the literature on the subject of political information. We begin this review with a discussion of the theory of information and product advertising in general, where lays the groundwork for the heart of our analysis in Chapter 3. The most important outcome of this literature, for our purposes, has been the classification of products by the type of information consumers seek. A bridge is developed between product advertising in general and its specific application to politics.

Product Advertising and Information Theory

The theory of product advertising parallels the theory of information. A highlighting of a few landmarks in information theory will help clarify some terminology used later. Stigler (1961) made an early contribution to the theory of information that is important for our purposes. He emphasizes the active search for price information by economic actors. Specifically, Stigler looks at the determinants of price search for individuals in the marketplace. The amount of search undertaken depends upon the distribution of prices that individuals estimate as they engage in search. If the sampled distribution has a large variance, more search is relatively attractive because the probability of finding a lower price is increased. If the sampled distribution has a small variance, more search is less likely to turn up a lower price. In Stigler's model, only one type of good exists, that is, a search good.

Nelson (1970, 1974) extended Stigler's seminal analysis and concentrates more directly on product advertising. His theory evaluates products in terms of quality as well as price. In addition, individuals obtain information both by active search and by more passive means. Nelson separates products into two types, search goods and experience goods. The distinction is made on the basis of the kind of information that consumers seek about a product. Consumers make this distinction because of the costs of obtaining information about a product prior to purchase. Nelson defines search goods more narrowly than Stigler. Goods for which information is inexpensive to gather prior to purchase are search goods. This includes information on price and quality. Consumers are able to find out and compare actual qualities of search goods prior to purchase. Goods for which information is more costly to gather prior to purchase are experience goods. Consumers evaluate the qualities of experience goods after purchase. These qualities are not known to consumers prior to purchase. In reality, very few goods are entirely search or experience. Rather, most goods have characteristics of both types of goods. A continuum exists between the polar cases of search and experience. Most products fall somewhere along this spectrum. The distinction is a convenient simplification that allows products to be grouped according to the costs of search.

The distinction between search and experience goods affects the information that producers supply in advertising. Product advertisers respond to the information that consumers seek. For search goods, consumers seek to compare specific characteristics of products. Producers stress "direct information" in advertisements for search products. Direct information describes specific characteristics of the product. Information contained in advertisements for search goods accurately portrays the quality of the product. Consumers can relatively costlessly compare advertised qualities to actual qualities prior to purchase. Opportunities for producers to increase profits by deceptive advertising are minimal because of the nature of search goods.

The information contained in advertisements for experience goods has caused some debate in the literature. The basic idea presented by Nelson is that for experience goods, consumers do not actively seek to compare specific characteristics before purchase. Advertisements for experience goods contain "indirect information". Indirect information focuses on the brandname and past reputation of the product rather than on specific performance characteristics. Advertisements for experience goods essentially identify a producer as a source of current and past supplies and attempt to validate the reputation of a producer of high quality products. Advertisements for cars are often of this type. The product is often identified with an easily recognizable and trusted personality or the name of the product is exhibited in a way to make it easy to remember.

The advertising of experience goods serves as a signal to overcome the lack of specific information that consumers can effectively obtain. Many of the situations discussed by Akerlof (1970) involve purchases of goods or services that are experience goods or services. In these cases an asymmetry exists between the information possessed by sellers and purchasers of a product. Akerlof notes that in many instances, institutions have developed which signal consumers of quality and alleviate some of the asymmetry. These institutions include brand names and chain or franchise sellers. The seminal work in the area of brandnames as signaling devices is Spence (1973).

Unlike search goods, advertisements for experience goods may not always contain truthful statements. Nelson suggests that an incentive may exist for producers of experience goods to lie about their quality in advertisements. They are able to do so because the costs to consumers of becoming informed about specific qualities prior to purchase are high. Producers might be able to deceptively advertise, gain sales, and increase profits relative to truthful advertisements. Nelson does not believe this incentive carries the day. He and Ferguson (1976) state that repeat purchases of higher quality goods lead them to be advertised truthfully and more heavily. They assume that because of the higher quality product, high quality producers will obtain more repeat purchases than producers of low quality goods. Sellers of higher quality goods will advertise accurately more heavily because the present value of a trial purchase is higher. If this return were not present, higher advertising expenditures would not pay. Nelson's argument hinges on this asymmetry of return on advertising between low and high quality producers. With search goods, consumers compare the quality of goods prior to purchase so that higher advertising expenditures will not necessarily convey higher quality. Johnsen (1976) came to the same conclusion by assuming some consumers to be "experimenters". The "experimenters" try highly advertised products. They recommend products with high quality to other consumers, who in turn purchase the highly advertised high quality products.

Several articles have put Nelson's and Ferguson's conclusion that higher quality goods are advertised more on a sounder foundation. In the process these articles also substantiated the assertion that experience goods producers use brandname and reputational advertising. Telser (1980) develops a model of self-enforcing agreements, where the only "punishment" for cheating is the loss of future transactions. The incentive to produce promised quality is operative as long as a positive probability of future transactions exists. Klein and Leffler (1981) use their model of self-enforcing contracts to more explicitly address advertising. They point out that Nelson's reasoning on quality and advertising is circular. High quality sellers advertise more because of repeat purchases, and consumers repeat purchases only because goods are advertised. Instead, Klein and Leffler state that investment in advertising indicates a conspicuous investment in non-salvagable brandname capital. This type of investment signals consumers of higher quality. The ability to invest in these projects shows the existence of a price premium that allows higher quality production. The non-salvagable aspect of the investment signals consumers that short-run quality deception would be less profitable to a firm. The firm could not recover the cost of the investment. The distinction from Nelson's work is subtle. In Nelson's work, higher return on advertising pays the higher quality firms to advertise more. In Klein and Leffler's model advertising signals higher quality, but there is only a normal rate of return on the fixed investment.

Kihlstrom and Riordian (1984) develop a model similar to Klein and Leffler's. Advertising is a conspicuous signal that high quality firms have cost and demand functions such that they can afford more advertising. They have two variants of their model. In the first, even low-advertising producers of high quality products gain reputations in the long run. Advertising pays only if it increases fixed costs and not marginal costs. In the second variant, low-advertising producers never gain a reputation. Advertising is effective even if low quality firms have fixed and marginal cost advantages. This variant is closely related to Klein and Leffler.

Schmalensee (1978) arrives at an opposite conclusion. He notes that high quality brands also have relatively high unit costs. These costs may mitigate the gains from advertising. This is especially true when consumers hold a universal belief that advertising implies quality. This belief leads to more purchases but reduced market shares for high quality producers. However, to obtain this result, he assumes optimization by sellers but not full optimization by buyers.

The important features of this advertising literature can be briefly restated. Goods are lumped into two categories: search goods and experience goods. Consumers actively compare prices and qualities of search goods. Qualities advertised for search goods correspond to actual qualities. Higher advertised search goods are not necessarily of higher quality. Experience good advertising will stress brandname and reputational aspects of the seller and be a non-salvagable cost. Incentives exists for producers to misrepresent the quality of experience goods in advertisements by advertising heavily. In general, however, higher advertised experience goods signal higher quality.

Product Advertising as Political Advertising

The product advertising models discussed above lay an important ground-work. However, our interest is not so much with product advertising in general as it is with the more specific analysis of political advertising. One branch of analysis in political advertising simply applies the product advertising models from the last few pages to politics. Nelson (1976), Telser (1976), and Ferguson (1976) are in this class. Specifically, Nelson states that political advertisements contain primarily direct information, that is, information about specific characteristics of candidates. Candidates' service records are available. Voters can compare the actual records with the promises of candidates. Political advertisements will contain truthful statements because voters can easily detect dissonance between the advertised message and past performance. This implies that legislative services are search goods. Voters compare detailed characteristics of candidates before voting.

Telser and Ferguson disagree with Nelson. Telser views political services as experience goods because it is difficult for voters to draw inferences about the future behavior of candidates. Political services are not like search goods. Voters cannot gain specific knowledge about the future performance of candidates. The voters must rely on the brandname or past reputations of politicians. Ferguson acknowledges the availability of the records of incumbents. Voters, though, have little incentive to find, check, and compare these records to the promises contained in advertisements. The benefits to any single voter are small, while the costs of investigating candidates' records can be high. Nelson has ignored this incentive problem that faces voters. Nelson states that while voters do not have an incentive, opposing candidates have the incentive to provide information about the past performance of their opposition. However, a credibility problem exists when a challenger presents the information about his opponent. Voters must filter this information and assign some probability to the truthfulness of the message. The incentive problem is only moved back one step. Now, voters must acquire information about the credibility of the charges made by a candidate about his opponent.

Technology And the Costs of Campaigning

A second branch of analysis of political information that we review does not rely so much on extensions of specific product advertising models. Instead, more general economic concepts and models are used to analyze the effects of changes in technology and political spending. Abrams and Settle (1976) demonstrate that technology in the form of television affects the costs of political campaigns. The growth and spread of television has had a net effect of reducing the cost of advertising in presidential campaigns. Allowing for other influences, as television expands into more households, candidates spend less to reach their targeted audiences. Television lowers the cost of transmitting a message to voters. In essence, the introduction of television creates a technological externality that reduces the cost of political campaigns. The lower cost function reduces the price of campaign messages and increases the quantity demanded of campaign messages.

The debate over the effectiveness of political advertising and campaign spending still continues. The extent to which political campaign advertising increases vote returns is unsettled, although a considerable literature has accumulated on the subject. We take the time to only highlight some of the work. Palda (1975) uses data from elections in two Canadian provinces. His two samples confirm one another. Campaign spending by candidates had a positive impact on their vote totals. Palda breaks spending down into mass media expenditure and expenditures on personal expenses and finds both to increase vote returns. These results hold up when he uses predicted expenditures from a regression to explain per voter expenditure by candidates. Changing the dependent variable to measure the share of votes instead of vote levels did not alter the basic result. Welch (1974) also uses a simultaneous equation technique and also finds a positive relationship between campaign spending and vote totals.

Jacobson (1978, 1980) presents evidence that only campaign spending by non-incumbents has a positive influence on election outcomes. He uses a simultaneous equation technique and finds that an increase of 10,000 dollars in spending by a non-incumbent increases his vote percentage by one and one-half points in U.S. House races. In a 1976 article, Welch attempts to find the effect of money on votes regardless of incumbency. He finds a positive but diminishing effect of expenditures on votes, when the influence of incumbency is controlled. Later, Welch (1981) criticizes the specification of Jacobson's model. Jacobson fails to provide a variable in his expenditure equation that will identify it from the vote equation. Welch runs an identified model for the 1972 House elections and finds a significant but weak effect of non-incumbent spending on votes. An increase from 10,000 dollars to 58,000 dollars in spending increases a challenger's vote by only two percentage points.

As is easily seen by the brief survey above, the estimation of the effects of campaign spending is plagued by many problems. Jacobson (1985) surveys some of these problems. One problem is the simultaneity problem. Money influences votes, but incumbency and voting behavior in office also influence contributions. This problem has at least been partially addressed by simultaneous models. A second problem within this literature is the difficulty of separating the effects of challenger and incumbent spending. Obviously, both variables can be entered into a regression equation; however, the correlation between the two variables prevents a valid estimation of the separate effects. A variable is needed that controls for the strength of the incumbent and challenger before any money is spent. Suffice it to say, money influences vote production, but the exact magnitude of the effect is still unclear in the empirical literature.

The product advertising analogies to political advertising and the more general applications of economic theory to political information markets leave us with some basic and important conclusions. Most simply, voters respond to information changes. We can, however, go far beyond this statement. Voters will seek more, and completely new types of information given changes in the costs of obtaining information.

The Rational Voter Model

Both the theoretical and empirical work on political advertising discussed so far presume that the information available to voters and/or changes in that information set affect the way people vote. This presumption, however, has a solid theoretical foundation. The rational voter model as developed by Downs (1957), Tullock (1967), and Riker and Ordeshook (1968) provides the theoretical framework. The rational voter model views the decision in terms of a cost-benefit calculus by the voter. Both the probability of voting for a particular candidate and the probability of voting at all are predictable, using this framework. The likelihood of voting for a candidate depends on the benefits to the voter times the probability of influencing the outcome, minus the costs of voting. The costs include both the "out-of-pocket" costs of driving to the polls and of obtaining information about the candidates, as well as the opportunity costs of taking the time to become informed and to vote.

The most important feature of the model for our discussion is the inclusion of the costs of voting in the decision calculus. As with any activity that individuals value, changes in the price of the activity will affect the amount consumed by individuals. Voters respond to changes in the cost of voting and when the cost of voting decreases, economic theory predicts that more voting will occur. Also, to the extent that voters value information about candidates, reductions in the cost of obtaining information will induce voters to become better informed.

Several writers have found empirical support for the rational voter model. Frey (1971) stated that the observed higher voter participation rates of higher income classes stems from the effects of information. Higher income individuals can participate more efficiently in the voting process than can lower income individuals. An investment broker can think about projects en route to and from the polls, while an assembly worker must completely stop work. Downs (1957) concluded that the participation difference was due to the lower information costs to higher income individuals. The individuals tend to be better educated so that the cost of information is lower. These types of arguments have had critics. Tollison and Willett (1973) assert that Frey's point may be qualitatively correct but is most likely empirically insignificant. If voters have no or very little information about candidates, Tollison and Willett agree with Downs' point. However, the introduction of more information where information is already plentiful may not increase voter turnout. Instead, it may make candidates more difficult to distinguish, and thereby reduce the benefits of voting. Tollison, Crain, and Pautler (1975) show that increases in information that are provided relatively costlessly by television and newspapers help to explain voter participation. Increases in information on television and in newspapers lower the costs to voters of becoming informed. Ashenfelter and Kelley (1975) used several measures of the costs of voting. They found the costs of voting to have negative effects on voting. The strongest of these variables was the poll tax that was used mainly in southern states to keep blacks from voting. In addition, literacy tests had a negative effect on voter turnout.

Televised Legislatures

Most of the literature specifically about televised legislatures has occurred in the news media. These sources mainly surveyed the emergence of television. A few articles have speculated about possible effects.

Detailed analysis of televised legislatures is sparse. Garay (1980) describes some of the political factors on U.S. congressmen prior to the introduction of television. The House wanted to improve its visibility and public image. Also, improvements in camera technology made coverage less cumbersome. The Congressional Research Service (Stevens 1977 and Rundquist and Nickels, 1986) has conducted the most extensive study of televised legislatures to date. The 1977 CRS study assesses television coverage at the state and international level. It concluded that the coverage was, in general, nondestructive to legislative processes. The 1986 study focused on the impact of televised Senate sessions on Senate floor proceedings. The most significant change in the proceedings was an increase in the number of Special Order speeches. This is attributed to a reduction on the maximum length of a Special Order speech. The old limit was 15 minutes. The new limit is 5 minutes.

Other articles that do not deal directly with televising legislative sessions have, nonetheless, analyzed television news coverage of Congress and the effects of that coverage. Robinson and Appel (1979) studied the extent and nature of network news coverage of Congress. They used seventy-five news programs of the three major networks over a one month period in 1976. The networks devoted over twenty percent of the news time to the U.S. Congress. Of this amount, fifteen percent was about congressional matters other than campaigns. Further, coverage of the Senate doubled the time spent on the House. This last piece of data is related to a study done by Peabody, Ornstein, and Rhode (1976). They attribute the increasing domination of presidential candidacy by senators relative to congressmen to the extra exposure that senators receive over congressmen.

History of Televised Legislatures
In the United States televised coverage of state legislatures began several years before the U.S. House opened its doors to cameras. The Congressional Research Service (Stevens, 1977) conducted a survey of televised state legislatures during the mid-seventies. In 1970, Georgia initiated daily coverage of its legislature. By the mid-seventies almost half of the state legislatures had some form of daily coverage. The daily coverage was most often 30-minute to 60-minute edited programs with taped segments from the day's floor and committee sessions. The states with infrequent coverage mainly covered special addresses and events within the legislature.

Internationally, by the 1980s more than twenty national legislatures permitted television coverage of floor proceedings. Many countries began the practice during the early days of television in the 1940s and 1950s. Since that time, the trend has been toward coverage in more countries. Once adopted, no national legislature has eliminated television coverage. Several countries, such as Canada, Japan, and the United States televise all or almost all of the official debate. Other national assemblies televise only major debates and debates about the future of the government. The French National Assembly is an example of this type of coverage. In many respects the U.S. Congress has lagged behind the other democratic countries with regard to television coverage of the legislative process.

The debate in the U.S. Congress over television has a long history. The first motion for televised House sessions came in 1944, and this motion was defeated solidly. Formal committee hearings on the idea of television coverage were held in 1965 by the Joint Committee on Organization of the Congress. During the 1970s, the tide for televised sessions grew steadily. In the 93rd Congress (1973-74), the Joint Committee on Congressional Operations began a two-year study of televising Congress, and a report was released in October 1974. The standard concerns about "grandstanding" were voiced by congressmen, fearing that the public would get a distorted picture of the reality of Congressional business. These concerns delayed the adoption of television until October of 1977, when the U.S. House passed House Resolution 866. This resolution eventually allowed cameras into the House chambers.

House Resolution 866 supported television coverage but delegated the details of the implementation and operation of coverage to the Speaker of the House. The House Speaker at that time was Thomas P. (Tip) O'Neill (D-MA), who had become Speaker in that same year. The resolution also called for a special *ad hoc* committee to give recommendations about coverage to the Speaker. Before H. Res. 866, the Speaker conducted a 90-day trial coverage of House business, carried only to House offices. The House permanently implemented coverage in 1978, although the telecasts were carried only over a closed circuit to the offices of the House members for the next year and a half. The public gained access to the House telecasts in April 1979, when C-SPAN began live, gavel to gavel telecasts of regular House business.

While the telecasts were provided by a private service, control of the cameras was retained by the House, itself. For example, cameras were only allowed to show representatives engaged in debate at the podiums. In effect, the Speaker of the House was given the authority over the operation of the cameras.

Controversy over television cameras in the U.S. House did not end once they were introduced. A few Republican congressmen began to use the after regular business hours, "Special Orders," sessions to make extended partisan speeches in front of the cameras and an empty House chamber. The Democratic leadership took notice of these speeches as the media paid more attention. The Speaker of the House finally ordered the cameras to pan the empty chamber during the Special Orders speeches. A heated debate the next day resulted in the first reprimand of a Speaker by the House since 1797 (Cohen (1984) and Granat

(1984) provide summaries of these episodes. After the "Camscam" incident, the Democratic leadership set up a committee to examine the effects and uses of the coverage. After the committee's report, the Speaker adopted a favorable attitude toward the coverage.

In the Senate, the debate over television started at the same time as in the House. Senate Resolution 66 to permit coverage reached the Senate floor in 1984 due to the support of Majority Leader Baker (R-TN). The resolution was filibustered to death by Senator Russell Long (D-LA) and other Senators, who expressed concerns that television coverage in the Senate would lead to larger problems in the Senate than in the House, because of procedural difference between the two chambers. Debate on issues is not limited in the Senate as it is in the House. This difference in the rules would allow for more show-boating opportunities in the Senate than in the House.

After the defeat of Senate Resolution 66, support for television coverage grew among senators. Minority Leader Robert Byrd (D-WV) did not support the resolution sponsored by Majority Leader Baker because it would have allowed gavel to gavel coverage. In 1985, Byrd sponsored his own resolutions (S. Res. 2, S. Res. 28, S. Res. 29) that would have permitted television coverage but would have limited coverage to times when the leadership of both parties agreed to it (Bonafede, 1984, and Blakely, 1985 detail these developments.) In March of 1986 the Senate adopted a revised version of Senate Resolution 29. The resolution allowed cameras into the Senate for a trial period, beginning in the summer of 1986 and mandated a vote on permanent coverage after the test period. In July of 1986, the Senate voted to allow coverage on a permanent basis.

These episodes convey a clear message—televised legislatures illicit keen interest and passionate responses from legislators. At the outset of television in the House, the Speaker of the House, Thomas O'Neill, was not a strong supporter of televised sessions. In fact, he was opposed to coverage. As the coverage increased the House's visibility relative to the Senate's, he became a supporter. Senate Minority Leader Robert Byrd summarized the shift in visibility when he said, "The Senate is fast becoming the invisible half of Congress" (Blakely 1984). Former Senate Majority Leader Howard Baker stated that until the Senate adopted coverage, "the Senate will continue to be unable to hold our own with respect to media coverage at the White House and in the other body" (Cohen 1985).

Legislators are not alone in their preoccupation with televised legislative sessions. The evidence collected on viewership of the sessions suggests that the coverage also stimulates interest among voters. Cohen (1985) reports the results of a poll of C-SPAN viewers. By 1984, about 40 million households received the

Table 1
C-SPAN (House) and C-Span II (Senate) Penetration by State

State	C-Span Subscribers in State	C-Span II Subscribers in State	Basic Cable Subscribers in State	%C-Span	%C-Span II
AL	274,662	58,000	585,140	47	10
AK	56,775	0	65,687	86	0
AZ	333,709	157,187	433,424	77	36
AR	165,327	41,000	374,182	44	11
CA	2,803,880	1,066,370	3,852,268	73	28
CO	382,860	240,074	491,430	78	49
CT	620,255	204,727	699,511	89	29
DE	21,123	18,000	135,845	16	13
FL	1,569,461	397,229	2,362,940	66	17
GA	405,183	157,879	897,081	45	18
HA	168,114	0	216,030	78	0
ID	109,836	32,630	154,447	71	21
IL	1,086,019	333,924	1,339,446	81	25
IN	493,716	116,931	840,477	49	14
IA	318,935	90,700	434,409	73	21
KS	458,945	91,780	581,270	79	16
KY	396,222	187,693	626,396	63	30
LA	375,753	16,315	725,699	52	2
ME	72,978	0	192,806	38	0
MD	411,735	109,855	463,241	89	24
MA	891,420	203,320	956,086	93	21
MI	1,049,960	161,247	1,243,111	85	13
MN	336,686	207,919	474,927	71	58
MS	83,824	43,630	444,703	19	10
MO	478,240	132,600	549,803	87	24
MT	121,442	0	144,509	84	0
NE	185,390	112,770	298,148	64	39
NV	86,010	0	136,007	63	0
NH	170,601	13,000	189,165	90	7
NJ	1,130,583	279,958	1,389,670	81	20
NM	137,978	85,362	226,683	61	38
NY	1,983,706	418,685	2,406,025	83	17
NC	430,945	153,130	920,082	47	17
ND	29,131	0	119,738	24	0
OH	1,281,567	321,458	1,807,189	71	18
OK	386,372	138,178	545,657	71	25
OR	301,782	77,000	484,666	62	16
PA	992,223	242,106	2,053,229	48	12
RI	170,609	19,814	176,158	97	11
SC	263,475	9,630	430,300	61	2
SD	79,022	0	104,337	76	0
TN	379,994	102,781	702,415	57	15
TX	1,730,666	921,723	2,426,368	71	38
UT	74,009	2,251	148,997	50	2
VT	61,344	4,731	87,349	70	5
VA	755,749	166,904	927,730	81	18
WA	516,886	83,397	758,344	68	11
WV	89,680	0	410,825	22	0
WI	424,127	121,102	626,150	68	19
WY	46,552	17,111	118,386	39	14
TOTAL	25,250,654	7,594,842	36,881,998	68	21

telecasts of the U.S. House of Representatives. Of these households, 38 percent watched their legislators at least one hour per month. This number increased by 11 percent from 1982 to 1984. Roughly, 13 percent watched at least 20 hours per month. Assuming two voters per household, over 15 million tuned in to the coverage on a monthly basis. To put this in perspective, that is about one-fourth of the total number of voters in the 1984 presidential election. A 1986 study of C-SPAN viewership supplies even more insight into both the U.S. House and Senate broadcasts. Table 1 shows the results of this survey of C-SPAN penetration into cable markets by state. The table lists the number of subscribers to the House and Senate broadcasts in each state, the number of basic cable subscribers in each state, and the number of House and Senate subscribers as a percent of total subscribers. In eight states 1 million subscribers received the U.S. House telecasts. In total in 1986, over 25 million cable subscribers received the House broadcasts. The Senate telecasts, because of their relative newness, penetrated fewer households. However, close to 8 million subscribers received the Senate broadcasts. In addition to the live coverage, almost all voters are exposed to the coverage through short, taped segments shown on nightly news telecasts across the country.

Summary

Developments in the theory of product advertising and political advertising have implications that will be of use in the following chapters. The literature we have surveyed in this chapter leaves us with several important points. First, voters respond to changes in information. Both the theoretical and empirical work in this area tend to support this conclusion. Second, the type information that voters seek and use, direct or indirect, depends on the costs of obtaining the information. Finally, a technological change that affects the information gathering ability of voters alters political variables. The succeeding chapters use these basic points to derive and test several hypotheses about the impact of televised legislatures on election and legislative outcomes.

Chapter 3

LEGISLATIVE TELEVISION:
THE TRANSFORMATION OF POLITICIANS

> *Learn your lines, don't bump into the furniture and, in*
> *kissing, keep your mouth closed.*
>
> Ronald Regan advising Senators in 1986 on how
> to deal with televised coverge of the Senate.

Television increases the information available to voters. This assertion appears obvious and unobjectionable. A more interesting and debatable question is how this change in information alters voter behavior? How is the politician transformed in the voter's mind by the innovation of legislative television?

The previous chapter discussed the effects of informational changes on the behavior of consumers in general and voters in particular. That literature leads us to expect responses by voters to changes in cost of acquiring information. Also, it lays a theoretical groundwork that can be applied to the specific case of televised legislatures.

How does televising legislatures affect the reelection of incumbents? A simple hypothesis is that more legislative exposure provides free advertising for incumbents and will work towards their reelection. We develop an explanation of the effects of televised legislatures on election outcomes in this chapter. Our hypothesis goes beyond the obvious point that televising legislatures increases voter information about incumbents. Our interest lies in the type of information provided in televised sessions and in the responses of different types of constituencies to more information about legislator behavior. Our conclusion is that incumbents will sometimes be helped by coverage and will sometimes be hurt by coverage.

The chapter is organized as follows. The second section briefly discusses the distinction between search and experience products. The types of information provided in advertisements for search and experience goods are the main focus of attention. The third section extends the search versus experience distinction to the advertising of political services. We identify the circumstances in which televised sessions will help or hinder incumbent reelection. The fourth section discusses the effect of a technological advance such as televised sessions on the cost of acquiring information. This has implications for the type of information voters will seek and on the outcome of incumbent reelections. The fifth section summarizes the chapter.

The Relationship Between Citizens and Politicians

Economic analysis of political information is not new. Much of the literature has developed the "rational ignorance" theme, i.e., a voter has little incentive to become informed about politics because the expected benefits of an individual's vote is trivial. The focus has been on why voters will not expend many resources to become informed. To the extent voting occurs, voters want to discover candidate qualities at the least cost.[1] Changes in information and the cost of information will illicit responses by voters.

Two processes concerning how voters determine the qualities of political candidates are suggested in the literature on product advertising. Products are classified according to which of the two processes is the most efficient way for consumers to evaluate quality.[2] The product categories are search products and experience products. The titles of the two categories provide cues to their meanings. Search products are those for which it is cheaper to compare actual qualities to advertised qualities prior to purchase. Experience products are products for which the actual qualities are not known to the buyer until after the purchase. It is cheaper to discover the qualities of experience products in other ways, learning brandnames and reputations, for example.

As discussed in the second chapter, the distinction between search and experience products is important because it affects the type of information contained in product advertisements. The information contained in advertisements for search products is primarily "direct information" and the advertising content of experience products is "indirect information." Direct information describes specific characteristics of the product and indirect information identifies the product's brandname and past reputation. Search product advertisements contain direct information because the consumer is making up his mind prior to purchase so he seeks specific characteristics to compare. The indirect information contained in experience product advertisements will stress the identity of the product and the longevity of the brandname because specific qualities about the product will not be detected prior to purchase. For experience products, higher advertising levels signals higher quality. For search products, the level of advertising is not necessarily a signal of higher quality; in some cases it is a sign of lower quality. Search product advertising will convey accurate information because consumers will recognize inaccurate information before buying and are less likely to purchase. With experience products, repeat purchases help to insure advertised quality but some false advertising of product quality may occur.

Political Services and the Content of Political Advertising

The analysis of commercial advertising can be extended to political advertising. Quality is important in politics, and voters, like consumers, want cost-effective information. Voters want to obtain political information and to evaluate candidate qualities in the most frugal way. Political services will be evaluated differently depending on whether they are more like experience products or like search products.

Political services will be more like experience products if it is costly for voters to compare the advertised qualities of the candidates to actual qualities prior to voting. The lower the cost of evaluating candidates before the election, the more political services will be like search products.

If political services are experience services and advertising contains indirect, brandname information, incumbents will have an advantage for two reasons. First the better financed candidates will be more successful and incumbents tend to be better financed. Like the commercial product analogy, voters interpret the more heavily advertised politicians as better buys. Second, the fact that the incumbent has a brandname in his office and, in most cases the challenger does not, helps the incumbent. If political services are search products, candidate advertising contains more direct information, and more heavily advertised candidates are not necessarily at an advantage. Larger expenditures on direct information advertising can cause voter backlash. For example, suppose voters recognize that political advertisements are appealing to or financed by contributions from special interests. A plausible voter response is to vote against the candidate who advertises the most. That candidate would be the most indebted to special interests. Also, where voters actively seek information, as they do with search goods, incumbents are less able to target specific interest groups. An adverse voter reaction to more direct information advertising is not expected in all cases. However, the possibility exists for adverse reaction.

Given direct information, the type of reaction voters have to more heavily advertised candidates depends on characteristics of the constituency. Consider two examples to illustrate. If the incumbent serves a homogeneous constituency, then his political message to voters is Johnny-One-Note. Johnny Representative from a farming district will promote and vote for pro-farmer bills in the legislature. Given an all-farm constituency, televised coverage of his legislative performance makes it cheaper for farmers to compare and verify his advertised claim. There is no dissonance because the live telecasts of the legislator reach the same interest group targeted in his political advertising. The messages from both sources are consistent and in their interest. At the other extreme, consider a district that contains diverse political interests. In order to appeal to different groups, campaign advertising will contain different messages and be targeted for specific groups. In a district composed of textile manufacturers as well as cotton farmers, more general exposure of the incumbent's position on import quotas will raise opposition. The more attention drawn to incumbents' positions, the more their reelection prospects are hurt.[3]

When political services are experience products, constituent diversity will not pose as great a difficulty for candidate advertising. Less attention will be concentrated on the candidate's specific policy positions because advertising will focus on information such as the candidate's committee seniority and experience.

Technology and the Relative Cost of Acquiring Political Information: Experience Versus Search

The relative cost to voters of acquiring information about the qualities of politicians is not independent of technology. Television has been an important technological change in the production of political information, not to mention commercial information.[4] Televising legislative proceedings lowers the relative cost of comparing the politician's advertised qualities with his actual qualities before the election. (One channel runs the politician's campaign advertisement; another carries his speech live from the chamber.) Voter comparisons between the advertised versus the actual qualities of legislators are relatively simple when legislatures are televised.[5] The television news media also monitor legislative broadcasts and use portions of the live proceedings that are of interest to the community. It is not necessary for the individual voter to watch gavel-to-gavel because the news programs have commercial incentives to be efficient monitors.

Televising live sessions changes the type of information voters seek from political advertisements. More direct information about the candidate would be sought in political advertising because the televised sessions make it cheaper for the voter to obtain information about a politician's actual legislative performance. When legislative sessions are not televised, it is more costly for voters to compare advertised information with the candidate's actual performance. Political services in this case are more like experience services, advertising is primarily indirect, voters perceive more heavily advertised candidates as a sign of better quality, and incumbents have the built-in advantage of having an established brandname in the office. With televised sessions political advertising contains more direct information, and more heavily advertised politicians lose their edge in retaining their seats when they represent diverse interest groups. In districts that contain relatively homogeneous interest groups, televised sessions make it cheaper for voters to verify the incumbent's advertised policy positions, and voters react positively to more candidate advertising.

Summary

Televising legislatures alters the process by which voters evaluate the qualities of political candidates. The cost of comparing advertised political qualities to actual qualities prior to the election is lowered. Political services are more like search products in televised legislative settings. In non-televised settings, political services are like experience products, and political advertisements stress brandnames and reputations. In televised legislatures, political advertisements will contain direct information about the candidates.

The impact of direct advertising by incumbents, relative to brandname advertising, depends on characteristics of the constituency. With diverse constituencies more direct information about policy positions creates opposition as well as support. In politically homogeneous constituencies, direct information about policy positions helps the incumbent candidate. The positions are more easily verifiable by televised sessions. The advertised message reinforces and is reinforced by the actual performance. More heavily advertised candidates will be helped by televised sessions when constituent interests are relatively uniform. The advantage of incumbents will be hurt by televised sessions when constituent interests are politically diverse.

Footnotes

[1] The economics of voting literature is surveyed in the second chapter. Some of the important articles are Tollison and Willett (1973), and Tollison, Crain, and Pautler (1975).

[2] See Nelson (1970, 1974).

[3] The discussion follows from questions raised in the exchange between Nelson (1976), Telser (1976), and Ferguson (1976).

[4] See Abrams and Settle (1976).

[5] This comparison between advertised and actual performance becomes even more viable when it is recognized that most final votes on legislation are taken near the end of the session, that is, close to election day. See Crain and Tollison (1980) and Crain, Leavens, and Tollison (1986).

Chapter 4

THE EFFECT OF TELEVISING LEGISLATURES ON ELECTIONS: THE CASE OF U.S. STATE LEGISLATURES

The analytical framework in Chapter 3 predicts that televised sessions will not be a blessing to all incumbents. Those from homogeneous constituencies will be the likely beneficiaries, while incumbents from heterogeneous constituencies will suffer from the increased exposure. This chapter takes these implications from the purely theoretical stage and examines them in light of data from actual televised legislatures. The most obvious competing hypothesis is that televised sessions simply provide another barrier to entry into politics. If our prediction is correct, the data should indicate a systematic correlation between constituent diversity, televised sessions, and incumbent victory rates. The alternative hypothesis predicts only that incumbent victory rates will be increased by legislative television.

We develop an empirical model of U.S. state legislative elections that allows these competing predictions to be tested. At the state government level, there are several types of television coverage. We have obtained complete data for 1976. At that date 44 states had experimented with televised legislative proceedings of one form or another. The types of television coverage adopted by the states are shown in Table 2.

Our empirical work in this chapter is organized in the following way. The next section posits an empirical model of the number of winning challengers in state houses as a function of televised sessions, constituent diversity, and other relevant variables. The model is estimated by ordinary least squares using 1976 data. The third section re-estimates the model, but with 1962 data. The purpose here is to determine if the 1976 results are due to "reverse causation," that is, did states with more diversity tend to be the ones that adopted television. The fourth section estimates a similar model for state senates. The fifth section offers some concluding remarks.

Table 2
Types of Television Coverage in State Legislatures*

State	Frequent	Occasional	Infrequent	None
Alabama	X			
Alaska				X
Arizona				X
Arkansas			X(House)	X(Senate)
California		X		
Colorado			X	
Connecticut	X			
Delaware			X	
Florida	X			
Georgia	X			
Hawaii	X			
Idaho	X			
Illinois		X(House)		X(Senate)
Indiana		X		
Iowa		X		
Kansas			X	
Kentucky	X			
Louisiana	X			
Maine	X			
Maryland			X	
Massachussetts		X(House)	X(Senate)	
Michigan			X	
Minnesota		X		
Mississippi				X
Missouri				X
Montana			X	
Nebraska	X(Senate)			
Nevada		X		
New Hampshire			X	
New Jersey		X		
New Mexico			X	
New York		X		
North Carolina		X		
North Dakota		X		
Ohio		X		
Oklahoma	X			
Oregon			X	
Pennsylvania		X(House)		X(Senate)
Rhode Island		X		
South Carolina			X	
South Dakota		X		
Tennessee		X		
Texas				X
Utah			X	
Vermont		X		
Virginia			X	
Washington	X			
West Virginia			X(Senate)	X(House)
Wisconsin	X			
Wyoming				X
Totals	13	17	15	10

*Notes: Unless otherwise noted both houses within the state have the same type of coverage. The determination of the coverage level was made, excepting Alaska, by the Congressional Research Service and presented in Arthur G. Stevens, "Television Floor Proceedings in State Legislatures," in *Senate Communications with the Public,* 111 (1977). The information for Alaska was obtained from the Washington Office of the Governor of Alaska.

The Advantages to Incumbency in Televised Legislatures:
State Lower Chambers

The empirical model used to distinguish between these alternative hypotheses is stated below:

$$\text{WINNING CHALLENGERS} = f[\text{TELEVISED SESSIONS, DISTRICT SIZE,}$$
$$\text{MULTI-MEMBER DISTRICTS, SEATS}$$
$$\text{UP FOR ELECTION].} \qquad (1)$$

The dependent variable, WINNING CHALLENGERS, measures the level of entry into the legislature. This is the measure of the degree to which live television coverage affects the advantage of incumbency. TELEVISED SESSIONS indicates the extent to which the state legislature broadcasts its sessions. Following the categories shown in Table 2, states are distinguished between the high exposure (coverage is frequent or occasional) versus the low or no exposure states. This variable is used to split the states into separate samples for estimation. Separate samples are called for because we test and reject the hypothesis that election outcomes in the two categories of states are samples drawn from the same population.

DISTRICT SIZE is self-explanatory. This variable is a proxy for political diversity. Seats with larger populations, on average, have more diverse interest groups. As DISTRICT SIZE increases, more challengers are expected to win in televised states relative to non-televised states. This follows because incumbents are less able to convert their fund raising advantage into an advertising advantage and they can less effectively target audiences. With a politically diverse constituency more opposition will arise to positions taken by the incumbent than without televised sessions, when he would be able to run primarily on his political brandname. In the non-televised cases more advertising would signal higher quality, and incumbents can effectively target voters in their own advertisements. Fewer challengers would be expected to win in diverse districts when sessions are not televised. The alternative hypothesis predicts that fewer challengers would win in televised states, regardless of the population characteristics of the constituencies.

MULTI-MEMBER DISTRICTS is entered as a control variable. As the number of multi-member districts increases, more challengers win.[1] Single-member districting is the political counterpart to geographic division of commercial territories. Exclusive market separation is a collusive tactic to restrain competition. The function of segmenting political markets is to help incumbent efforts to restrain political competition. Single-member districts make entry into politics more difficult. In multi-member districts incumbents run in overlapping geographic territories and face an open market for voters. One incumbent can siphon votes away from another incumbent. In single-member districts, where residency requirements prohibit two incumbents from facing the same voters, there is less competitive incentive among incumbents. We expect a positive sign on this coefficient.

Finally, the number of SEATS UP FOR ELECTION will influence the number of challenger victories. The more elections that are held, the more opportunities challengers have to win. This is simply a control variable.

Table 3
Number of Winning Challengers in the State Houses, 1976

Independent Variables	Pooled Sample	No/Low Coverage States	High Coverage States
Constant	-4.961	-9.759	1.503
	(-1.63)	(0.17)	(0.333)
District Size	-0.000079	-0.00024	-0.000051
	(-2.47)**	(-2.33)**	(-1.88)*
Multi-Member Districts	0.241	0.355	0.107
	(3.52)***	(3.04)***	(1.48)
Seats Up For Election	0.334	0.327	0.270
	(13.68)***	(9.41)**	(7.69)***
Adjusted R Squared	.874	.938	.711
Sum of Squared Residuals	3400.7	1248.1	1125.6
F-Statistic (d.f.)	106.95***	97.26***	22.32***
	(3,43)	(3,16)	(3,23)
Observations	47	20	27

Notes: Alabama and Maryland were omitted from the pooled samples and subsamples because no elections were held. Nebraska was omitted because it is unicameral. Winning challengers for Kentucky, New Jersey, and Virginia are for 1977 election results while 1975 election data is used for Louisiana and Mississippi.

The Chow test F-statistic is 5.9l with (3,39) d.f. This rejects, at the .01 level, the hypothesis that the sub-periods are from the same population.

t-statistics are listed in parentheses.
*** – Significant at .01 level for two-tailed test.
 ** – Significant at .05 level for two-tailed test.
  * – Significant at .10 level for two-tailed test.

The data used to estimate the model are for elections to state houses and senates in 1976. The state house results are presented in Table 3 and the results are estimated on three samples. Column A reports the results when the entire (Pooled) sample is used; Column B is for states with No or Low television coverage; and Column C is for states with High Coverage. The division of the data samples into Low versus High Coverage states allows a test for structural differences in the two types of legislative environments. The Chow test of the null hypothesis that the two samples are from the same population was rejected at the one percent level for state houses.

The statistical analysis proceeds as follows. First, the findings for 1976 are described. Next, in order to distinguish between the hypothesis developed in the theoretical section and the alternative that television generally helps incumbents, the models are estimated using the same breakdowns for 1962, a period prior to the televising of legislatures. If the theory proposed is correct, differences found in the post-television era should not be present in the earlier period.

Figure 1
Effect of Population Per Seat on
Number of Winning Challengers, House 1976

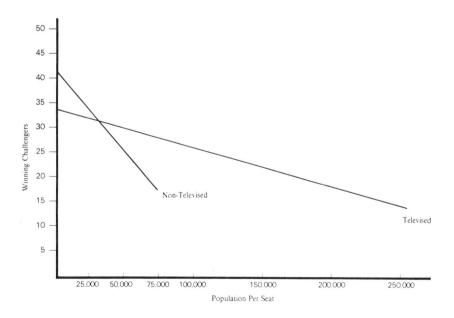

Note: The values for the schedules are computed by using the mean values for the variables for each sub-sample.

Of primary interest in Table 3 is the effect of DISTRICT SIZE on the number of winning challengers. For No/Low Coverage states the coefficient is negative and significant at the 5 percent level. In High Coverage states the effect is also negative and significant at the 10 percent level. These results are depicted graphically in Figure 1 in order to facilitate the discussion. DISTRICT SIZE is measured along the horizontal axis, and WINNING CHALLENGERS is measured on the vertical axis.

As illustrated in Figure 1, television coverage is an advantage for incumbents in states with small house districts. The number of winning challengers is less in televised than in non-televised states when voting populations are less than 49,000 per seat. For states with larger house districts (populations greater than 49,000 voters), television coverage of legislative sessions becomes a liability to incumbents. In large house districts challengers have a better chance of winning in televised states. Where constituencies are politically diverse, television exposure of an incumbent's actual legislative posture reduces his incentive to advertise and his brandname advantage.

Two points of reference will illustrate the difference between televised and non-televised states. First, consider a state with a population of 25,000 per seat and with televised legislative proceedings. The expected number of winning challengers is about 32, a 29 percent turnover rate. (See Figure 1.) In a comparable non-televised state about 37 challengers would win, a 32 percent turnover rate. Second, consider a televised state with a voting age population of 75,000 voters per seat, about 30 challengers would win. About 25 challengers would win in non-televised states with comparably large districts.[2]

The results for the control variables in Table 3 appear as expected. MULTI-MEMBER DISTRICTS is positive and significant. Comparing No/Low Coverage states to High Coverage states finds a large difference in the magnitude of this effect. The effect of MULTI-MEMBER DISTRICTS is over three times greater in low exposure states than in high exposure states. On average, 1 more incumbent loses for every 3 additional multi-member districts without televised house sessions. With televised house proceedings 10 additional multi-member districts result in 1 more incumbent loss. The difference is explained by a reduction in the amount of "cheating" activity among incumbents as a result of broadcasting their legislative conduct. Actual legislative performance is subject to discipline by the party leadership, which means that party members are not prone to open criticism of other members on the floor.[3] Televised sessions broadcast this congenial image from the halls of the state capitol, which means that rivalry on the campaign trail is dampened. In contrast, when the image of a working relationship among party members is not broadcast to voters, the rivalry on the campaign trail among incumbents competing for the same voters is intensified. Multi-member districts result in relatively more incumbent defeats in non-televised states. Finally, as expected, SEATS UP FOR ELECTION is positive and highly significant.

Test For Reverse Causation

The 1976 results for state houses indicate that there are differences between televised and non-televised states. Specifically, the difference involves the effect of constituent diversity (DISTRICT SIZE) on the advantage of incumbents. If this interpretation is correct, this same systematic difference between the two types of states for a period before televising legislatures started should not be found. Alternatively, if the same difference holds up for the earlier period, this would suggest that it is not television but something else that is driving the 1976 results. For example, suppose state legislators are more likely to adopt television where incumbents are less likely to be reelected because telecasts increase their likelihood of reelection. The 1976 findings alone are not sufficient to reject this alternative hypothesis. If the decision to televise was caused by higher incumbent turnover rates, turnover might be lowered in these states after television, even though turnover remained higher than in non-televised states.

The appropriate statistical comparison is to see if the difference between televised versus non-televised states was smaller in the post-television period than in the pre-television period. The test of this alternative hypothesis for state houses is contained in Table 4. The model estimates the results for 1962, a period prior to legislative telecasts. Not all of the data on the MULTI-MEMBER DISTRICT variable used in the 1976 model are available for 1962. The same model, except this variable, is used in Table 4. The results are re-estimated for 1976 and compared to the 1962 findings. In both periods the same groupings of the televised versus non-televised states are used. Note that the 1976 results without the MULTI-MEMBER DISTRICT variable are virtually identical except for a slight reduction in the adjusted R squared. Again, we are able to reject (at the 1 percent level) the null hypothesis that in 1976 there is no difference between televised versus non-televised states. In 1962, the pre-television period, the null hypothesis cannot be rejected. In the pre-television period there is no systematic difference in the number of challengers that won; turnover in state legislatures that subsequently adopted telecasts was not different than turnover in the other states. This finding rejects the competing hypothesis that television generally helps incumbents, and that states with higher turnover were simply the ones that adopted television.

State Upper Chambers

The results for state senate elections are presented in Table 5. The findings for

Table 4
Test for Reverse Causation in State Houses

Independent Variables	1976			1962		
	Pooled Sample	No/Low Coverage States	High Coverage States	Pooled Sample	No/Low Coverage States	High Coverage States
Constant	-5.272 (-1.34)	-0.849 (-0.160)	3.356 (0.76)	2.945 (0.612)	2.44 (0.32)	4.033 (0.53)
District Size	-.000097 (-2.77)***	-.00034 (-2.83)***	-.000059 (-2.14)**	-.000086 (-1.50)	-.00011 (-0.54)	-.000091 (-1.39)
Seats Up For Election	0.374 (15.33)***	0.400 (13.27)***	0.272 (7.56)***	0.339 (10.50)**	0.338 (7.85)***	0.339 (6.44)***
Adjusted R Squared	.841	.908	.697	.705	.761	.612
Sum of Squared Residuals	4378.3	1966.9	1232.7	10,160.2	4074.2	6040.8
F-Statistic (d.f.)	122.6*** (2,44)	95.24*** (2,17)	30.85*** (2,24)	56.04*** (2,44)	31.20*** (2,17)	21.50*** (2,24)
Observations	47	20	27	47	20	27

Notes: Alabama and Maryland were omitted from the pooled samples and subsamples because no elections were held. Nebraska was omitted because it is unicameral. Winning challengers for Kentucky, New Jersey, and Virginia are for 1977 election results while 1975 election data is used for Louisiana and Mississippi.

For 1976, the Chow test F-statistic is 5.03 with (3,41). This rejects at the .01 level, the hypothesis that the sub-periods are from the same population. For 1962, the Chow test F-statistic is .06 with (3,41) d.f. The hypothesis that the sub-periods are from the same population cannot be rejected.

t-statistics are listed in parentheses.
*** – Significant at .01 level for two-tailed test.
** – Significant at .05 level for two-tailed test.
* – Significant at .10 level for two-tailed test.

state senates are consistent with our house findings. We note that MULTI-MEMBER DISTRICTS variables are not included in Table 5 because it was not significant. For the 1976, post-television, period the null hypothesis that the two types of states are taken from different populations is not rejected (See Table 5). In the pre-television period, 1962, the two samples of states are significantly different at the five percent level. In 1962, states that subsequently adopted television had lower incumbent turnover than states that never implemented television. In 1976, turnover in the televised legislatures was statistically no different than the other states. This is exactly the opposite result that one should find if television protects incumbents, and that those states with the most vulnerable incumbents were the ones to televise.

In short, while the results for state senates do not provide much additional support for our basic hypothesis, they are particularly discouraging for the alternative hypothesis that television generally benefits incumbents. Challengers in state senates that have televised their sessions have benefited relative to their chances of winning in the pre-television period.

Summary

This chapter has developed a model of the effects of televised legislative sessions on election outcomes. The results for state legislative elections indicate that the effects are not independent of characteristics of the districts. For state house races television coverage benefits incumbents serving small, politically homogeneous constituencies. In larger, more diverse constituencies televised house sessions benefit challengers. In state senate races challengers generally have benefited from televised senate proceedings relative to the pre-television era. The competing hypothesis that televised sessions are simply a form of free advertising that generally helps incumbents is rejected by the findings.

The framework for the analysis is an extension of the theory of information and product advertising. Televising legislative sessions is a technological change that lowers the cost to voters of comparing the advertised to the actual qualities of the candidates prior to the election. This results in a different type of information being sought by voters in campaign advertising. Politicians respond to voter demands by stressing more specific, direct information in their advertising. This contrasts to the advertising of indirect information in the non-televised settings. Voters are more prone to evaluate the quality of political services after the election, like consumers do for experience products. The type of information contained in political advertising determines when an incumbent politician is better off by limiting his advertising. The analysis predicts the political conditions in which televised sessions would make incumbents more vulnerable.[4]

Table 5
Test for Reverse Causation in State Senates

Independent Variables	1976			1962		
	Pooled Sample	No/Low Coverage States	High Coverage States	Pooled Sample	No/Low Coverage States	High Coverage States
Constant	5.402	1.229	8.63	3.150	6.60	3.13
	(3.37)***	(0.58)	(3.69)***	(1.40)***	(3.59)	(0.80)
Population Per Seat	0.0000008	0.000006	-0.000002	-0.000005	0.000016	0.0000099
	(0.14)	(0.61)	(-0.24)	(-0.48)	(1.37)	(-0.68)
Seats Up For Election	0.177	0.313	0.096	0.325	0.013	0.339
	(3.85)***	(4.42)***	(1.56)	(4.86)***	(1.69)*	(3.89)***
Adjusted R Squared	.226	.493	.023	.331	.014	.370
Sum of Squared Residuals	801.5	223.5	478.5	1761.3	219.8	1210.0
F-Statistic	7.43***	9.77***	1.291	1.9***	1.138.65***	
(d.f.)	(2,42)	(2,16)	(2,23)	(2,42)	(2,16)	(2,23)
Observations	45	19	26	45	19	26

Notes: Alabama, Hawaii, Maryland, Michigan, and Virginia did not hold elections in 1976. Observations for Kentucky, New Jersey, and Virginia are for 1977, and Louisiana and Mississippi are for 1975.

For 1976, the Chow test F-statistic is 1.80 with (3,39) d.f. The sub-periods are statistically from the same population. For 1962, the Chow test F-statistic is 3.01 with (3,39) d.f. The hypothesis that the sub-periods are from the same population can be rejected at the .05 level.

t-statistics are listed in parentheses.

*** – Significant at .01 level for two-tailed test.
** – Significant at .05 level for two-tailed test.
* – Significant at .10 level for two-tailed test.

An explanation for why U. S. House proceedings were televised much sooner than Senate proceedings is suggested by the analysis. In addition to being smaller, U.S. House districts are revised periodically to conform to new census data. Redistricting maintains relatively more homogeneity. Senators serve larger, state-wide constituencies that cannot be adjusted in response to demographic changes. Televised sessions would likely reduce the electoral advantage of U.S. Senators because of the diversity of their constituencies. Based on the findings presented here, more U.S. Senators will lose in each election with the Senate coverage. We return to this topic in more detail in Chapter 7.

Footnotes

[1] See Crain (1977).

[2] The difference between the coefficients on DISTRICT SIZE in low/no versus high coverage state is significant at the .001 level.

[3] The strength of the incentives that legislators face from party leaders is substantial as demonstrated by Leavens (1984).

[4] This suggests that previous empirical models of the relationship between campaign spending and election outcomes suffer an omitted variable problem. See Jacobson (1980) and Welch (1981). Omitting constituent diversity in statistical modeling fails to control for differences in the incumbents' incentives to outspend opponents. This could explain the peculiar result in this literature (even using simultaneous equations techniques) that higher incumbent spending is correlated with lower incumbent vote percentages.

Chapter 5

THE EFFECTS OF TELEVISED LEGISLATURES ON ELECTIONS:
THE CASE OF THE U.S. HOUSE OF REPRESENTATIVES

The effects of televised sessions on incumbent reelection at the state level were tied directly to constituent diversity. We now turn to the estimation of the effects of legislative television on U.S. House elections. The results are consistent with the state findings. U.S. Representatives from homogeneous districts increased their election margins after television coverage relative to representatives from heterogeneous districts.

Televised coverage of U.S. House proceedings was first made available to the public in April 1979. These broadcasts were and continue to be carried by C-SPAN, a privately owned cable TV company. The date of introduction means that almost all of the House proceedings of the 96th Congress were broadcast live, gavel-to-gavel. The diversity hypothesis from the third chapter predicts that the coverage will help congressmen from homogeneous districts in elections after 1979 relative to congressmen from diverse districts. The next two sections of this chapter test this hypothesis using data from the 1978 and 1980 congressional elections.

The main difference in estimating the effect at the national level is the measure of diversity. Because all U.S. House districts contain roughly the same population per district, this proxy that was used at the state level is a constant across congressional districts. In place of population per district, we measure diversity by differences in educational attainment among the constituency. The second section uses ordinary least squares to estimate the change in vote between 1978 and 1980 as a function of diversity and other variables. The third section sets up two equations to estimate the levels of vote for incumbents in 1978 and 1980 and imposes cross-equation restrictions. This separates and clarifies the effect of diversity in each of the elections. The fourth section offers some concluding remarks.

U.S. House Races: Before Versus After TV

To examine the effects of television on congressional vote returns, it is necessary to compare election returns from the pre-television era to those after television. The last election prior to the introduction of television occurred in

1978, and the 1980 election was the first election after the House became televised. The effects of televised sessions probably increased after 1980 as C-SPAN expanded into more local cable networks and congressmen took fuller advantage of the coverage. Therefore, we would expect the differences in before versus after to increase over time. However, statistical comparisons of the 1978 House electoral returns to elections after 1980 is complicated by the nationwide congressional redistricting after the 1980 census (comparable election data for specific districts is a problem).[1]

Equation (2) presents the empirical model used to test the diversity hypothesis at the national level:

$$DVOTE = f[DED, DOEXP, DREP, VOTE78]. \qquad (2)$$

The dependent variable, DVOTE, is the difference between an incumbent's vote percentage in 1980 and his vote percentage in 1978. Observations are used only where the winner of the 1978 election ran for reelection in 1980. This isolates the effects of television upon legislators affected by the coverage in 1979.[2] In seats where the incumbent did not run for reelection in 1980, we do not expect television to change vote returns. This reduces the total observations in use from 435 to 386. The maximum increase in vote for an incumbent was 48.4 for Marvin Leath from Texas and the maximum decrease was 51.8 for John Jenrette from South Carolina.

DED, the measure of constituent diversity, is the variable of central interest. DED measures the degree of educational diversity in a constituency. It is the percentage of a district's population with a high school degree or less, minus the percent with a college degree. DED is always a positive number. When DED is large, more of the district's population has a high school degree or less, that is, the district is homogeneous. Incumbents will benefit from television coverage. When DED is small, the number of people with a college degree is more equal to the number with a high school or less education. This means more diversity with respect to educational background. Incumbents will lose votes where DED is small. The expected sign for DED is positive. Increases in homogeneity will increase vote returns for incumbents in 1980 relative to 1978.

DOEXP measures the change in expenditures by opponents of incumbents. It is the percentage expenditure by challengers in 1980, minus the percentage expenditure by losers in 1978. One problem in estimating the effects of spending on votes is that the levels of incumbent and challenger spending very often move in identical directions. Also, absolute differences in incumbent and challenger spending can be misleading. For example, where an incumbent outspends a challenger by 50,000, dollars and total spending exceeds 500,000 dollars is not comparable to where a challenger spends one dollar and an incumbent 50,001 dollars. Differences in percentage expenditure yields a measure that takes relative differences in spending into account. Increases in DOEXP will decrease returns to incumbents. In other words, an increase in the percentage of total spending by the opponent in 1980 relative to 1978 will lead to a decrease in DVOTE.

DREP is a dichotomous variable equal to one if a representative is a Republican and equal to zero otherwise. This variable controls for the problem of comparing the non-presidential year election in 1978 to the presidential year election in 1980. In essence, we use this dummy variable to capture any "coattail" effects that accompanied the Reagan victory in 1980. Also, DREP measures the general increase in support for Republican candidates in 1980 relative to 1978. The expected sign is positive.

VOTE78 is the percentage vote for the winner in the 1978 election. In many cases the level of the vote for the winner in 1978 constrains variations in DVOTE. In the extreme case where the 1978 vote was 100 percent, DVOTE can only take values from zero to -100. The general point is that DVOTE is more likely to go down as VOTE78 increases; hence, the expected sign on VOTE78 is negative.

We estimate equation (2) by ordinary least squares. The results are in Table 6. Overall, the regression is significant at the 1 percent level and explains 45 percent of the change in vote from 1978 to 1980.

The measure of district diversity, DED, is positive and significant at the one percent level. In districts with voters of similar educational backgrounds, representatives gained votes between 1978 and 1980. An incumbent from a district where the number of high school or less constituents outnumbered college graduates by 40 percent gained over 3 percentage points relative to an incumbent where the DED was 20 percent, *ceteris paribus*. This result suggests that the introduction of television into the House in 1979 helped legislators from homogeneous districts.[3]

The coefficients on the remaining explanatory variables are significant for at least the 5 percent level. The change in percentage opponent expenditure, DOEXP, has a strong negative effect on the change in vote. In a district where an incumbent's opponent spent more in percentage terms in 1980, the vote return for the incumbent diminished. A 4 percent increase in expenditure by an opponent, as a percent of total expenditure, reduced a representative's vote by 1 percent, holding other variables constant. Membership in the Republican Party, DREP, increased in 1980. Reagan "coattails" had an impact in 1980. The return on Republican Party membership in 1980 amounted to almost 3 percentage points. VOTE78 has the expected negative and significant sign. Higher vote

Table 6
Changes in Votes for U.S. Representatives, 1978 to 1980

Independent Variable	Coefficient	t-Statistic
CONSTANT	9.702	1.984*
DED	0.159	2.808**
DOEXP	-26.555	-11.676**
DREP	2.726	2.466*
VOTE78	-0.350	-9.476**
R^2	.456	
F(4,381)	79.8**	
N	386	

Notes: * – significant at .05 level for two-tailed test.
        ** – significant at .01 level for two-tailed test.

returns in 1978 constrained DVOTE and made incumbent's votes more likely to decrease in 1980.

Test for Spurious Correlation

The results presented in the previous section do not specify what the relationship of DED was to the **levels** of vote in 1978 and 1980. The results in Table 6 only indicate that the effect of DED on votes increased in the 1980 election. A possible criticism of those results is that the proxy for diversity, DED, is correlated with other variables which affect vote production. The single equation OLS method used earlier does not specify what effect DED may have had prior to television.

We use a different estimation technique in this section to examine DED's effect in the two elections. First, we estimate an equation to explain vote production in 1978. Next, two 1980 vote equations are estimated:one as an ordinary least squares estimation, and one in which the coefficient on DED is restricted to its 1978 value. The relationship between DED and votes prior to television is made clear. Also, comparison between the coefficient on DED in 1978 and 1980 is possible. Finally, we compare the fit of the restricted 1980 equation to the fit of the unrestricted 1980 equation to to test the significance of the change of the coefficient on DED. The form of the two equations are given in equations (3) and (4):

$$\text{VOTE78} = f[\text{DED, OEXP78, DREP}] \tag{3}$$
$$\text{VOTE80} = f[\text{DED, OEXP80, DREP}]. \tag{4}$$

DED and DREP are defined exactly as before. The dependent variable, VOTE78, is the percent vote for winners of 1978 U.S. House races. The dependent variable in equation (4), VOTE80, is the percent vote for incumbent U.S. representatives in the 1980 election. OEXP78 is the percent of total expenditure made by the loser in 1978. OEXP80 is the percent of total expenditure made by the challenger in 1980.

We expect the effect of DED to differ between the two elections. The coefficient on DED in the 1980 equation is expected to be a larger number than in the 1978 equation, based on the results presented in Table 6. However, the sign on the coefficient in each period is unknown. In the case that DED did not have any influence on votes before television, its coefficient in the 1978 equation will not significantly differ from zero. For this case, the coefficient on DED in the 1980 equation will be positive. If the proxy for diversity influenced votes before 1980, the coefficient on DED in 1978 may be positive or negative. No sign is predicted, *a priori.* In any case, the coefficient on DED in the 1980 equation is expected to be a larger number.

The effects of opponent spending, OEXP78 and OEXP80, are expected to have similar influences on vote production. The predicted coefficients on both variables are negative. Higher spending by opponents reduces votes for the winners in 1978. Higher spending by challengers will also reduce incumbents votes in 1980. The dummy variable for Republican Party membership, DREP, will vary between the 1978 and 1980 equations. From the earlier results, the coefficient in 1980 is expected to be larger. However, this does not necessarily imply a positive sign on the coefficient in either period because the influence on DREP in 1978 can be negative.

We estimate equation (3) by ordinary least squares. The results appear in Table 7. The equation explains 45 percent of the variation in votes for winners in U.S. House races in 1978. Overall, the regression is significant at the 5 percent level.

The coefficient on the proxy for diversity, DED, is small and insignificantly different from zero. No statistical relationship exists between diversity, as measured by educational backgrounds, and the number of votes for winners in 1978 House races. Prior to television, DED had no effect. OEXP78, the percent of total expenditures by opponents of 1978 winners, has a negative coefficient.

Table 7
Votes to Winners in 1978 U.S. House Races

Independent Variable	Coefficient	t-Statistic
CONSTANT	79.515	15.380**
DED	0.029	0.476
OEXP78	-45.596	-16.944**
DREP	-3.118	-2.642**
R^2	.452	
F(3,382)	104.9**	
N	386	

Notes: ** – significant at the .01 level for two-tailed test.

The coefficient is significant at the 1 percent level. Spending by opponents reduced votes for winners. Every 1 percent increase in expenditures by opponents decreased winners' votes by almost ½ of a percentage point. DREP also had a negative and significant influence on votes in 1978. The magnitude of the coefficient means that Republican Party membership cost a winning candidate 3 percentage points, *ceteris paribus.*

The estimation of 1980 votes, VOTE80, is done by two methods. These results are shown in Table 8. The left column results of Table 8 are generated by an unconstrained, ordinary least squares estimation. The right column results are from a regression that constrains the coefficient on DED to zero. (Zero is the value taken by the 1978 DED coefficient.) The unrestricted equation explains over 46 percent of the variation in votes in 1980. The constrained equation explains almost 46 percent. Both equations are significant at the 1 percent level.

In the unconstrained estimation, DED is positive and significant at the 5 percent level. For 1980 House elections more homogeneity, measured by increases in DED, led to more votes for incumbents. In 1978, DED had no effect. District diversity began to influence votes over the period in which cameras entered the U.S. House chamber.

The percent of total expenditures made by challengers in 1980, OEXP80, had a negative and significant influence on vote production. The magnitude of the coefficient is almost identical to the 1978 coefficient for opponent spending.

DREP is insignificantly different from zero in the 1980 election. Republican Party membership in 1980 was not a disadvantage, as it was in 1978. However, membership did not increase the level of votes for incumbent U.S. representatives in 1980.

The restricted 1980 equation is for overall comparison with the unrestricted 1980 results. The F-Statistic for comparison of the relative fits of the two equations equals 4.02.[4] This is significantly greater than zero at the 5 percent level. In the unrestricted 1980 equation the coefficient on DED is allowed to take on any value. The restriction of DED to its 1978 value of zero significantly reduces the explanatory power of the equation. DED makes a significant contribution to the 1980 equation.

In sum, the estimation method used in this section clarifies the influence of diversity as measured by DED. Diversity had no influence on votes in 1978. In

Table 8
Restricted and Unrestricted Estimation of Votes for Incumbents in 1980

Independent Variable	*Unrestricted* Coefficient/ (t-Statistic)	*Restricted* Coefficient/ (t-Statistic)
CONSTANT	69.776 (14.115)**	79.52 (1.54)
DED	0.119 (2.007)*	0 0
OEXP80	-45.154 (-17.337)**	-46.070 (-4.75)**
DREP	-0.703 (-0.604)	-1.09 (-0.103)
R^2	.463	.457
F(3,382)	110.0**	107.5**
N	382	382

Notes: * – significant at .05 level for two-tailed test.
       ** – significant at .01 level for two-tailed test.

The F-Statistic to compare the fits of the two equations is 4.02 with (1,382) degrees of freedom. This is significant at the .05 level.

1980, House legislators from homogeneous districts gained votes relative to House members from more diverse districts. These results support the hypothesis that diversity coupled with television reduces votes. They also suggest that DED has no effect without television.

Summary

The results found in this chapter add to the evidence that televised legislative sessions have an impact on elections. The results along with the results from the last chapter support the analysis. In particular, the hypothesis that televised sessions and diversity reduce votes, and television and homogeneity increase votes for incumbents seems viable. U.S. representatives from homogeneous districts gained from televised sessions as did state legislators from homogeneous districts. Legislators from diverse districts, whether U.S. House members or state legislators, lost votes from televised sessions. Live televised sessions redistribute influence from some legislators and political groups to others. This further suggests why all legislators do not support televised sessions.

Footnotes

[1] One effect of redistricting is that a representative's contintuency after 1980 is not matched perfectly with the constituency which elected him in 1978.

[2] This is important because our interest is on the effects of television on any given legislator in office when television was instituted.

[3] A variable which measured percent cable penetration in a district was also used by itself and in an interaction with DED. The expectation is that where C-SPAN is received more, the effect of diversity or uniformity will be greater. No effect was detected. One reason for this is that only the interaction of cable and diversity will affect voters. Because both of these are continuous variables, their interaction does not make sense. The units on the interaction are percent squared.

[4] The F-Statistic is generated by the Restricted Least Squares command in *Soritec.*

Chapter 6

THE EFFECT OF TELEVISED LEGISLATURES
ON THE OUTPUT OF LEGISLATION

Critics charge that televised legislative sessions become studios for political campaigning. Normal legislative business cannot proceed as usual. Senator Russell Long and others used this argument to kill 1984 legislation that would have allowed live television and radio broadcasts of the U.S. Senate.[1] This argument sounds sensible, but exactly how does television change legislative proceedings? This chapter analyzes this question. The U.S. Senate began live broadcasts of its sessions in 1986, and over half of the state legislatures have implemented television. If television distorts normal legislative operations, distortions are all around us.

We focus on the effects of television on the internal operation of legislatures. The effect of live television on election outcomes is brought into the analysis at several points. We organize the analysis as follows. The second section offers a simple model of legislative output. The model provides a framework to predict a legislator's response to the introduction of television. The model has two main implications. First, incumbents will pass more legislation where television reduces their reelection probability. In a model in which incumbents produce votes by legislation and by media exposure, this is a substitution away from media exposure into more legislation. Second, sessions will be shorter in states where television makes incumbents more vulnerable. Adjourning earlier is a sensible response when more exposure through televised sessions becomes a political liability. In the states where television makes incumbent reelection more likely, the response is to stretch-out the sessions. The third section provides evidence, using state legislative data. The final section offers some concluding remarks.

A Model of Television and Legislative Outcomes

The previous empirical sections found that televised legislative proceedings reduced votes for incumbents from heterogeneous constituencies. They increased votes for incumbents from homogeneous constituencies. Rational legislators will attempt to minimize the costs or maximize the benefits of coverage by adjusting other variables under their control. A simple adjustment they can make is the amount that they appear on camera. Legislators can adjust the length of their sessions to take advantage of or reduce the effects of television coverage. In states with television and diverse districts, an obvious response is to shorten session lengths. This minimizes the negative impact that television has on the reelection prospects of incumbents. In televised and homogeneous states, legislators will lengthen sessions to take advantage of the benefits of television.

The production of votes by legislators can be thought of in terms that are familiar to economists. Namely, multiple inputs are employed to produce given levels of an output, which, in this case, is votes. Given a normal production function that depends on two inputs, (X and Y), increases in the price of X will cause producers to substitute away from X and into the now relatively less expensive input Y. (This is true as long as the inputs are not perfect compliments.) In the case of vote production, changes in technology that reduce vote returns cause legislators to shift away from television exposure and into legislative output. Changes in technology that increase vote returns cause legislators to substitute into more television exposure and out of some legislative output. In order to maintain a given level of votes, fewer bills need to be passed in the situations where television makes it easier for incumbents to get reelected.[2]

Empirical Estimation

The effects of legislative television on proceedings can be tested empirically, again using data on U.S. state legislatures. In those states that allow broadcasts, session lengths and legislative output will depend on how television affects voters. The impact of televised sessions is not uniform across states. It is tied to the diversity versus uniformity of constituencies in the states. In states where representatives serve small, politically homogeneous districts, television increases votes for incumbents. This result was verified in the preceeding chapters. In these states more legislation will be passed, and sessions will be shorter relative to the other states. In states that contain large, politically diverse districts, televised legislative proceedings reduce voter support for incumbents. Legislative output will increase and sessions will be shorter in response. In this second case the effect of technology on votes is negative.

The empirical estimation of the model involves a two equation system to explain legislative output and session lengths. The forms of the equations used to estimate the effect of television on legislative output and session lengths are:

BILLS PASSED = f[DISTRICT SIZE, BILLS INTRODUCED,
             SENATE TERM, BICAMERALISM,
             STATE EMPLOYEES]   (8)

$$\text{LENGTH OF SESSION} = f[\text{DISTRICT SIZE, BILLS PASSED,}$$
$$\text{COMPENSATION, RESTRICTIONS,}$$
$$\text{RECORDING METHOD]}. \qquad (9)$$

The fit values for the first equation, BILLS PASSED, will be used to explain session lengths in the second equation.

BILLS PASSED is the number of bills enacted during the 1975-76 biennium. The DISTRICT SIZE variable is the main variable of interest for testing the theory. DISTRICT SIZE is the average of the mean senate and house district size for each state. In states with large, politically diverse representative districts, legislatures will increase their output of legislation in response to the ill effects of television coverage. In states with small districts, legislation will be reduced as legislators shift more into exposure. In sum, the theory predicts a positive sign on DISTRICT SIZE for states with television coverage.

The other variables enter the output equation as control variables. BILLS INTRODUCED controls for the demand for legislation. It is a measure that attempts to capture the general level of demand by interest groups for legislative action without breaking that demand down into its specific components. More bills introduced into legislative debate indicate a higher demand for legislative output. The expected sign on BILLS INTRODUCED is positive. Increases in bills introduced will increase the number of bills passed.

SENATE TERM, BICAMERALISM, and STATE EMPLOYEES are supply side variables. SENATE TERM is a dummy variable for the length of a senator's term in each state. Senators are elected to term lengths ranging from two to four years in the states. SENATE TERM equals one, where term lengths are four years and equals zero, where term lengths are two years. The dependent variable, BILLS PASSED, covers a single biennium. Senators with four year terms face a time horizon over which to pass legislation that extends past a single biennium. Senators with two year terms face reelection at the end of each biennium. They have two years to work on and attempt to pass the legislative agenda that voters will evaluate at the next election. The senators with two year terms have incentive to pass more legislation over a single biennium. The sign on SENATE TERM will be negative. Longer terms lead to less output over a two-year period.

BICAMERALISM is the size of the senate divided by the size of the house in a state legislature. It controls for the differences in the constituent base between the two chambers. As the two chambers approach each other in size, the constituent bases of each chamber are more similar. This reduces the cost of agreement between the two chambers. Unequal chamber sizes implies different constituent bases and higher agreement costs between the chambers. The expected sign on BICAMERALISM is, therefore, positive.[3] STATE EMPLOYEES is the number of state employees per capita. No sign is predicted. On the one hand, more state employees may increase the amount of legislation passed because the larger bureaucracy means more information for legislators about the demand for legislation. On the other hand, the larger bureaucracies may increase the costs of passing legislation. More committee hearings are required to hear from the bureaus, and bureaus in many instances are competing for different legislative outcomes. In this case larger bureaucracies mean less legislation for a given time period.

The results of estimating equation (8) by ordinary least squares appears in Table 9. Three sets of results are reported: Low/No Coverage states, High Coverage states, and the pooled sample. Overall, the regression explains between 59 and 66 percent of the variation in bills passed. The F-statistics for the three equations are highly significant.

Table 9
Bills Passed in State Legislatures, 1975-76

Independent Variables	No/Low Coverage States	High Coverage States	Pooled Sample
CONSTANT	938.57	154.71	445.84
	(2.45)	(0.49)*	(1.67)*
DISTRICT SIZE	-0.19e-2	0.38e-2	0.28e-2
	(-1.14)	(3.93)**	(3.07)**
BILLS INTRODUCED	0.71e-1	0.11	0.71e-1
	(2.89)**	(3.57)**	(3.42)**
SENATE TERM	340.32	-579.35	-307.63
	(1.49)	(-4.21)**	(-2.45)*
BICAMERALISM	163.39	1316.65	1101.75
	(0.26)	(2.05)*	(2.27)*
STATE EMPLOYEES	-0.34	-0.68	-0.14e-1
	(-2.87)**	(-0.66)	(-1.58)
R^2	.623	.743	.555
F-STATISTIC	4.62*	12.14**	10.21**
(d.f.)	(5,14)	(5,21)	(5,41)
N	20	27	47

Notes: t-statistics are listed in parentheses.
    * - significant at .05 level for two-tailed test.
    ** - significant at .01 level for two-tailed test.
    The sample corresponds to the one used in Chapter 4.

In the states with television coverage, DISTRICT SIZE has a positive and significant coefficient. In states without television coverage, DISTRICT SIZE has a negative and insignificant coefficient. With television coverage, more diversity, as measured by district size, leads to more bills passed. A 10,000 person increase in district size increases the number of bills passed by 40. This result confirms the prediction of the theory. In states with diverse districts and television coverage, legislators are hurt by coverage. One response legislators make is to shift into the production of more legislation.

The signs on the other variables in the output equation are as expected. BILLS INTRODUCED has a positive and significant effect on the bills passed both in states with and without television coverage. The introduction of 100 extra bills increases the number of bills passed by 9 (the average of the two sub-sample coefficients). SENATE TERM is negative and significant in High Coverage states but is insignificant in Low/No Coverage states. States with longer senate term lengths have less legislative output per biennium than states with shorter senate term lengths. BICAMERALISM has a positive coefficient but is significant only in televised states. More identical constituent bases led to more output in these states. The variable for bureaucracy size, STATE EMPLOYEES, is negative and significant in Low Coverage states and is insignificant in High Coverage states. Larger bureaucracies slow down the legislative process. An increase of 1000 employees per capita decreased output by about 17 bills in televised states and by about 38 bills in states without television.[4]

The estimation of LENGTH OF SESSION, equation (9), uses the total number of days the legislature was in session in the 1975-76 biennium. The definition of DISTRICT SIZE remains the same. The DISTRICT SIZE variable is again the main variable of interest. In states with large, politically diverse representative districts, legislatures will adjourn sooner in order to avoid exposure. In states with small districts, televised sessions will be stretched-out in order to increase exposure. The theory predicts a negative sign on the DISTRICT SIZE variable.

The remaining four independent variables are entered as controls. BILLS PASSED is the fitted value from the preceeding estimation. BILLS PASSED controls for the size of the state's legislative agenda. When the number of laws enacted is held constant, the effect of television on the time spent passing a given number of bills can be isolated. COMPENSATION is entered to control for differing opportunity costs facing legislators. Legislators in states where pay inside the legislature is low, receive a salary below a full-time wage, so that they have incentive to end the session earlier. Where pay inside the legislature is high, legislators receive salaries that are closer to their outside earning possibilities. When "inside" pay is high, there is less of an incentive to cut the debate short.[5] RESTRICTIONS is a dummy variable that controls for constitutional and statutory restrictions on session lengths. RESTRICTIONS equals one, if a state legislature has its session length limited either by statutory or constitutional law and equals zero otherwise. These limitations will shorten sessions, even where the legislature is empowered to override the restrictions.[6] RECORDING METHOD is also a binary variable. It equals one, where calendar days are the metric of length, and it equals zero, where legislative days are the metric. When recorded days in session include days the legislature does not convene, recorded length will be greater and the RECORDING METHOD coefficient will be positive.

The data used to estimate the model are again for state legislatures in the 1975-76 biennium. The results are presented in Table 10. The variables are estimated on the three samples. Column A reports the results when the model is

Table 10
Session Lengths in State Legislatures, 1975-76

Independent Variables	No/Low Coverage States	High Coverage States	Pooled Sample
CONSTANT	171.20 (3.44)**	58.76 (2.13)*	92.92 (3.28)**
DISTRICT SIZE	-0.24e-3 (-0.80)	-0.42e-3 (-1.66)	-0.48 (-2.52)*
BILLS PASSED	0.29e-1 (0.63)	0.67e-1 (2.31)*	0.66 (2.03)
COMPENSATION	0.23e-2 (1.45)	0.32e-2 (2.76)*	0.29e-2 (3.31)**
RESTRICTIONS	-107.04 (-3.14)**	-40.28 (-1.80)	-65.22 (-3.46)**
RECORDING METHOD	35.37 (1.26)	26.42 (1.11)	50.91 (3.00)**
R^2	.647	.663	.594
F-STATISTIC (d.f.)	5.122** (5,14)	8.29** (5,21)	12.02** (5,41)
N	20	27	47

Notes: t-statistics are listed in parentheses. * - significant at .05 level for two-tailed test. ** - significant at .01 level for two-tailed test.
The sample corresponds to the one used in Chapter 4.

estimated on the sample of No or Low Coverage states; Column B is for states with High Coverage levels; and Column C is for the entire (pooled) sample of states. The estimated results for the High Coverage and Low Coverage sub-samples are significant at the 1 percent level and explain between 41 and 66 percent of the variation in session lengths.

The primary concern is with the effect of DISTRICT SIZE on session length in the High Coverage states versus the Low Coverage states. In Low Coverage states the effect of DISTRICT SIZE on session length is small and not statistically significant. In states without coverage DISTRICT SIZE bears no relationship to the number of days legislators meet. In High Coverage states the effect of DISTRICT SIZE on session length is negative and significant at the 12 percent level. The size of the effect is large in this case. Holding other things constant and figuring for an average district size of 50,000, legislators meet about 21 fewer days in states that have televised sessions.

The signs on the control variables in Table 10 appear as expected. In High Coverage states, the number of bills passed has the expected positive and significant effect on session length. Ten extra bills take the legislators between one-half to a full day to pass. In Low Coverage states, the effect is positive but statistically insignificant. Legislator pay, COMPENSATION, appeared as a positive influence on session lengths in the two sub-samples. An increase in pay of 10,000 dollars induces legislators to meet an extra 23 to 32 days. Constitutional and statutory limitations had the expected influence on session lengths. RESTRICTIONS is negative and significant in the sub-samples and in the pooled sample. An average of the coefficients for the two sub-samples implies that restricted legislators met two months shorter, *ceteris paribus*. The metric used for session length, RECORDING METHOD, had the obvious effect on recorded length. Where calendar days were used, recorded session lengths were about one month longer than where legislative days were used.

Summary

A model of the effect of televised legislative sessions on legislative outcomes, namely, bills passed and session lengths, was developed in this chapter. The model indicates that the effect of television on legislative output and session lengths is not independent of the characteristics of legislative constituencies. Large, politically diverse districts and television coverage result in more legislative output and shorter sessions.

An explanation of the effects on legislative business of live television coverage in the U.S. House of Representatives and Senate is suggested by the analysis. In contrast to the received opinion, televising the House proceedings gives representatives from diverse districts the incentive to speed up the floor business of the House rather than to bog it down with grandstanding.

Footnotes

[1] For example, Rep. John B. Anderson (IL) stated that the House TV system is "...one more incumbent protection device at the taxpayer's expense". [It will] distort and prolong our proceedings by encouraging more and longer speeches for home consumption". (Cooper, 1979)

[2] A simple mathematical model of television's effects upon legislative output can be derived from the results presented in the preceeding chapters. Suppose session lengths are a function of bills passed (B) and technology (X). Mathematically,

$$T = T(B,X), \tag{5}$$

where $T_B > 0$, $T_{BB} > 0$, $T_X > 0$, and $T_{XX} < 0$. (Subscripts denote partial derivatives.) The empirical results on televised sessions and election outcomes help to sign T_X. When technology (X) increases votes (V), legislators will increase session lengths, or $T_X > 0$. When technology decreases votes, legislators will decrease session lengths, or $T_X < 0$. Session lengths will move in the same direction as votes, when technology changes.

By assumption, the objective of legislators is to maximize their vote returns (V). In the model developed here, the production of votes depends on three variables: bills passed (B), time in session (T), and technology (X). Expressing this functional relationship mathematically and substituting equation (5) for time in session yields

$$V = V[B;T(B,X);X], \tag{6}$$

where $V_B > 0$, $V_{BB} < 0$, $T_B > 0$, $T_{BB} > 0$, $V_T > 0$, and $V_{TT} < 0$. Based on these assumptions and the effect of technology on session lengths, the effect of technology on legislative output can be determined. Taking the total derivative of equation (6) and solving for dB/dX with dV = 0 produces

$$dB/dX = -(V_X + V_T \cdot T_X)/(V_B + V_B \cdot T_B) \tag{7}$$

Because V_B, T_B, $V_T > 0$, the sign of (7) depends on the signs of V_X and T_X. As discussed earlier, if $V_X > 0$, then $T_X > 0$ and if $V_X < 0$, then $T_X < 0$. This means that if technology has a positive effect on votes (V_X, $T_X > 0$), increases in technology lead to fewer bills passed, that is, $dB/dX < 0$. Conversely, if technology has a negative effect on votes (V_X, $T_X > 0$), increases in technology lead to more bills passed and $dB/dX > 0$.

[3] Crain (1977), McCormick and Tollison (1981), and Buchanan and Tullock (1962) discuss the effects of bicameralism.

[4] The substitution of income per capita for state employees per capita does not affect the equation and income per capita is not significant.

[5] The focus here is on the "inside" pay of legislators. The higher the inside pay, the higher is the opportunity cost of adjournment. McCormick and Tollison (1981) also analyze the opportunity cost effects on legislators. Their analysis centers on the "outside" pay of legislators. The higher the outside pay, the higher is the opportunity cost of remaining in session.

[6] Many of these restraints can be avoided by a two-thirds or three-fourths majority vote of the legislature. Although extension is possible in these cases, the costs to remain in session are higher. The majority required to remain in session must be secured.

Chapter 7

THE POLITICS OF ADOPTING TELEVISED SESSIONS

Why do legislators adopt television coverage? The legislators themselves have proposed several reasons, during the debates over televised sessions. Some U.S. Representatives and Senators viewed the public's "right to know" about its government as reason enough to support coverage. Others, as we quoted in Chapter 1, expressed concern over the loss of visibility in the upper chamber versus the lower chamber. The other side of this question, obviously, is why do some legislators vote to bar cameras from legislative sessions? Again, if we listen to the legislators, we hear concerns expressed for voters. John Anderson said that the House TV system represented, "...one more incumbent protection device at the taxpayer's expense." To listen to some politicians would lead us to believe that they have the good of the legislative process at heart. Senator Russell Long and others have voiced concern over TV's effects on legislative business. They expect politicians to grandstand and slowdown legislative business.

Public choice analysis is wary of uncritically accepting the rhetoric of politicians. Instead, public choice applies a simple but fundamental assumption to the behavior of politicians: legislators choose alternatives to maximize their personal objectives. This is the basic assumption made by economists about the behavior of individuals in other behavioral contexts. As in all of economics, these governmental agents face constraints on their behavior. With the constraints in mind, legislators weigh the personal costs and benefits of pending legislation. The case of televised legislatures should be no exception. To the extent that legislators anticipate the effects of coverage on their vote production, their support for coverage will be altered. The earlier chapters estimated the impact of televised sessions on elections. In this chapter we look at how the election effects and other influences change support for and dissent on televised sessions. In effect, we want to go beyond the rhetoric and consider the self-interest motivations that lie behind televised sessions.

The next section discusses the factors that operate on the self-interest of legislators in their decision to adopt television coverage. Two sets of factors are discussed: those that have similar effects on all legislators in a chamber, and those that have differential effects on legislators within a chamber. In the third section we set up an empirical model of support for televised sessions. The model is tested with data drawn from the July 1986 U.S. Senate vote, in which the senators voted to allow cameras inside the chamber on a permanent basis. The findings confirm that the senators are, indeed, concerned about the personal benefits and costs of coverage. The fourth section offers some concluding remarks.

Political Influences on Legislators

Two sets of influences on the decision to televise legislatures can be distinguished: 1) the factors that affect the chamber more or less as a whole, and 2) the factors that have different effects on legislators within the same chamber.[1] The relative importance and visibility of one legislative chamber to another is a factor that impacts the entire chamber. Legislators, whether state or national, are often candidates for other and higher offices. The legislative chamber serves as a training ground for these legislators. State representatives and senators become governors and U.S. Representatives. U.S. Representatives become U.S. Senators. U.S. Senators become President. These types of career movements fill the biographies of politicians in the U.S. Legislators also move from legislative chambers to bureaucratic and cabinet appointments in state and national government.

Television exposure that benefits one chamber relative to the other increases the mobility of the legislators in the benefited chambers. Televised sessions are one means by which the members of a chamber can increase their exposure and influence relative to the other chamber. The U.S. House is a case in point. The names of Gingrich and Walker became household names due to the C-SPAN coverage of the U.S. House. Before televised sessions they would have been two relatively unknown members of the minority party. The 1986 Senate resolutions on televised sessions (S.Res.2, S.Res.28, S.Res.29) were pushed mainly as measures to restore the visibility of the Senate. The opportunity to increase exposure relative to the other chamber supplies one incentive in favor of coverage.

Another factor that operates on a chamber more or less as a whole is the increased visibility relative to the executive branch. The executive branch has used television coverage to its advantage for a long time. This is especially true at the national level. Television news conferences, televised addresses, and constant news coverage of day to day activities of presidents have contributed to an increase in the power of the presidency relative to Congress. The public simply has had greater access to the views and proposals of presidents than it has had of the Congress. If a president meets a foreign dignitary, undergoes a medical examination, or spends a weekend at Camp David, television cameras cover the departure, return, and every incidental activity. Televised coverage of legislative sessions is one way the Congress can compensate for the visibility advantage of the presidency. This is a reason for adoption of television into the U.S. House.[2]

A third factor in the decision to televise is the demand for information by voters and interest groups. A general increase in the demand for information in governmental activities took place in the 1970s and continues. The Freedom of Information Act is one example. Although the sources of the push for more information on government may come from self-interested groups, the fact remains that the public has gained more access to the behavior of government. On the issue of televised congressional sessions, a 1977 Roper Poll showed that 68 percent of the public favored televised sessions.[3] As the demand for information from voters or interest groups grows, legislators have an added incentive to allow cameras into their chambers.

The incentives just disussed help us understand why a legislature adopts coverage, but they do not explain why a legislative body would drag its feet. Why do some lawmakers oppose coverage and why, for instance, did the U.S. Senate hesitate to install cameras? The answer must lie in factors that vary between politicians in the same chamber. Such factors will include the effects of television on the electoral returns of legislators. Also, personal characteristics that are specific to each legislator will figure in their decision.

Politicians will base their decision on televised sessions on how TV changes their vote production. Chapters four and five demonstrated that TV's effects on votes depends on constituent diversity. Incumbents in homogeneous districts are helped; incumbents in heterogeneous districts are damaged. We expect that the effects of diversity on support for TV will differ among legislators in similar fashion. To the extent that legislators from homogeneous constituencies recognize the benefits of coverage on their vote productions, they have an incentive to vote in favor of televised sessions. In contrast, legislators from diverse constituencies, who realize the costs of coverage on their vote production, have an incentive to vote against televised sessions. The prediction is straightforward. In a vote to televise legislative sessions, legislators from more homogeneous constituencies are more likely to vote for television than are legislators from diverse constituencies.

Characteristics of individual legislators will also determine support and dissent on televised sessions within a legislative chamber. For instance, length of service will influence the support of a legislator for two reasons. First, older legislators, who developed their political skills before televisions's impact became so large, will use television less effectively than younger legislators.

Younger legislators will have concentrated more heavily on using television to their advantage throughout their political career. Second, as in the case of Walker and Gingrich, the seniority system can sometimes be bypassed by skillful use of television. Lawmakers, who have spent a lifetime in building a reputation will not support a technological move that allows younger lawmakers to gain the same amount of visibility in a fraction of the time.

The distance between the ideology of a specific legislator and the leaders of a chamber will also affect the decision to support television. Legislators with very deviant views from the leadership may expect television to cast a bad light on them, when the cameras are controlled by the leadership. The leadership can manipulate the agenda and debate so as to promote the views of the majority of legislators.

Finally, the security of a legislator's job will influence his support for televised sessions. Legislators do not fully know and cannot perfectly anticipate all of TV's effects. If politicians are risk averse, those legislators with perennially wide victory margins will be less hesitant to adopt coverage. A legislator, who is uncertain of the effects and with a small winning margin, is likely to shy away from coverage.

Empirical Model of Support for Television in the U.S. Senate

The most recent vote at the national level concerning televised legislative sessions took place in the U.S. Senate in July 1986. The vote grew out of Senate Resolution 28, sponsored by Minority Leader Robert Byrd. In February of 1986, the Senate voted to allow television into the Senate chamber on a 90-day trial basis and to consider TV on a permanent basis at the end of the trial period. With the passage of the July 1986 resolution, the Senate provided for gavel to gavel coverage of Senate proceedings on a daily and permanent basis. The resolution passed by a vote of 78 to 21. In addition to TV coverage, the resolution continued the rule changes that were passed along with the trial coverage in February. The most substantive rule change shortened the length of time allowed for each "Special Order" speech. The Senate Special Orders session is similar to the one in the House, which stirred so much controversy.

With little doubt, the reason that Resolution 28 succeeded in the Senate where others had failed was due, in large part, to the factors operating on the Senate as a whole. Senators recognized the increasing prominence of the House from the visibility that TV permitted for the House. Also, with the increasing popularity of the House telecasts, constituent demand for Senate coverage began to increase. However, even in the 1986 votes, not all senators supported coverage. Over 20 percent opposed it. To get a handle on why some senators supported coverage and others did not, we must turn to the influences that vary across senators. Based on these factors, we set up the following empirical model to test the effects of diversity and legislator-specific variables on the probability of support:

$$VOTE = f[DED, YELECT, LVOTE, CCV, PCTWC, D86] \tag{10}$$

The dependent variable, VOTE, is a binary variable equal to one if a senator voted in support of permanent television coverage and zero, if he voted against coverage.

DED is the measure of diversity. As in the Chapter 4, it is the percent of the constituency with a high school education or less, minus the percent with a college degree. In this chapter DED corresponds to a senator's state instead of a representative's district. Uniformity increases as DED increases, and diversity increases as DED decreases. More uniformity among voters in a state is expected to increase the probability of support for television. In this case the vote production of legislators is increased by televised sessions. More diversity is expected to decrease support for television because the legislator's vote production will be damaged by coverage. The predicted sign on DED is positive.

YELECT is the year in which a senator was first elected to the Senate. Some of the strongest opposition to televised sessions has come from the older members of the Senate. For example, the senator responsible for a filibuster of an earlier resolution, Senator Long, has the longest tenure of any senator. Younger senators have developed their political skills in an era in which televised campaigning was essential. By contrast, Senator Long became a senator when television was still in its infancy. The younger senators will tend to use television to their advantage more easily than the older senators. The sign on YELECT will be positive. The more recent that a senator has been elected, the more likely he is to vote for televised sessions.

LVOTE measures the percentage of the vote obtained by a Senator in his last election. A senator who obtained only 50.1 percent of the vote is much closer to the margin of victory or defeat than is a senator who last gained 100 percent of the vote. Because televised national legislatures are still a recent event in the U.S., the effects may not be fully understood. Rational action does not imply full information. To the extent uncertainty exists, risk averse senators will avoid television. This effect is expected to be stronger, when a senator is closer the election margin. For senators far from the margin, any unforseen negative effects will impose much less of a cost. This predicts that senators with more votes in their last elections are more likely to support televised coverage. LVOTE will be positive.

CCV is the absolute value of the difference between a senator's conservative coalition ranking and the ranking of the Majority Leader, Robert Dole. As such, it measures the amount of deviance between a senator's ideology and that of the Senate leadership. We expect, with other effects held constant, that more deviance lessens support for television coverage. The likelihood of using TV to one's advantage becomes less as a senator's views become more extreme. The expected sign on CCV is negative.

Although the demand for information will affect a legislature as a whole, some constituencies will have a greater demand than other. We include PCTWC, the percent of a state's labor force employed in white collar jobs, as a proxy for the demand for information. The demand for information is usually considered to be income elastic. Because white collar jobs are associated with higher incomes, PCTWC captures this effect. PCTWC also measures the increased demand for information associated with higher educated classes. We, therefore, expect a positive sign on the percent of a state's labor force that is white collar. A higher white collar percentage will increase the probability of a senator voting in favor of televised sessions.

The dummy variable, D86, is equal to 1, if a senator faces reelection in 1986 and zero otherwise. Passage of permanent TV coverage in July 1986 would have affected senators in the 1986 election first. With some uncertainty as to television's effects, risk averse senators first affected by the coverage have a higher probability to vote against televised sessions. Senators up for reelection in 1988 and 1990 can analyze the effects in 1986 and adjust the coverage, if necessary. The expected sign on D86 is negative.

Equation (10) is estimated by ordinary least squares. In the estimation, we find that allowing for a diminishing effect of LVOTE and CCV provides a better fit. Therefore, we have included LVOTE and CCV along with LVOTE squared and CCV squared. Two specifications are estimated. Specification (A) does not include D86 and specification (B) includes D86 from the equation. These results appear in Table 11. With a dummy dependent variable, the R^2 is biased downward. However, it is reported. As measured by the R^2, the two specifications explain about 25 percent of the support for televised sessions. Overall, both equations are significant at the one percent level.

The diversity measure, DED, has the expected sign. The coefficient on DED is positive, indicating that more homogeneity increased the probability of a vote for coverage. However, the coefficient is not significant at standard levels. These results lend support to the idea that legislators consider the election effects of TV before voting on coverage. The fact that the magnitude of the effect is rather small may indicate that senators do not fully anticipate the effects of diversity and TV coverage on election outcomes.

The remaining explanatory variables have the expected signs and are

Table 11
Support for Television in the U.S. Senate

Independent Variable	Coefficient (t-statistic) (A)	Coefficient/ (t-statistic) (B)
CONSTANT	-7.636 (-3.00)***	-7.307 (-2.80)***
DED	0.010 (0.84)	0.010 (0.84)
YELECT	0.018 (3.27)***	0.017 (3.17)***
LVOTE	0.162 (2.87)***	0.158 (2.64)***
LVOTE^2	-0.001 (-2.87)***	-0.001 (-2.68)***
CCV	-0.020 (-2.12)**	-0.019 (-2.06)**
CCV^2	0.001 (2.29)**	0.001 (2.22)**
PCTWC	0.026 (1.70)*	0.027 (1.70)*
D86	-0.053	(-0.61)
R^2	.249	.253
F-STATISTIC (d.f.)	4.37*** (8,92)	3.85*** (9,91)
N	100	100

Notes: * - significant at .10 level for two-tailed test.
 ** - significant at .05 level for two-tailed test.
 *** - significant at .01 level for two-tailed test.

significant with the exception of D86. The year a senator was first elected, YELECT, is positive and significant at the 1 percent level. Younger legislators are more likely to support television coverage. LVOTE and its square show a positive and diminishing effect. Both are significant at the 1 percent level. Bigger winning margins cause senators to accept TV more easily. Deviance from the leadership's positions, CCV, is negative and significant at the 5 percent level. The square of CCV indicates a diminishing effect. Senators with more extreme views were less likely to vote for coverage. The proxy for the demand for information, PCTWC, is positive and significant at the 10 percent level. Senators from states with a large percentage of white collar workers were more likely to vote for coverage. D86 is negative but not significant.

Summary

While the effect of diversity on senators votes did not appear to be large, the model just estimated makes one point clear; Senators vote their self-interest. This can be seen in the fact that diversity does have an effect on votes. It is also and probably more conclusively seen in the other variables. The length of service, vote margin, and extremity of views had very clear and significant effects on Senators' votes. All of these variables capture some element of self-interest.

Footnotes

[1] For a more complete examination of these time-varying incentives for televised sessions, see Garay (1980).

[2] See Garay (1980).

[3] See Sisk (1977).

Chapter 8

MODERNITY

Live legislative television has introduced an innovative way for voters to make up their minds about electing legislators. Voters rely less than in the past on reputations or name recognition to decide which candidates are most likely to possess the qualities they desire. The qualities of incumbent candidates are displayed by legislative television as incumbents go about their daily legislating. Importantly, voters are treated to a live, low cost, demonstration of the political product before making a choice at the polls.

The shopping habits of voters have been changed by televising legislative action and, as a result, a new type of information about candidates is sought. Legislators have been transformed in the minds of voters from experience into search products and candidates have responded with different advertising messages. The effect of this chain of causation is to alter the electoral advantages of incumbent candidates, which has been a primary focus of our analysis and empirical evidence.

Stemming from the altered states of incumbent reelection prospects are a number of secondary adjustments. The conduct of legislative sessions and the amounts of legislative output have adjusted to the new voter-legislator relationship that has been created by legislative television. Adjustments in elections, sessions, and legislation are all observable consequences of televised legislatures.

There are abstract adjustments to which we now turn that are relevant to the broader issue of assessing the performance of the political system. Although these changes are conceptual, they are the most important for evaluating constitutional rules in light of changes in political information technology. The discussion will lead us into some specific directions for constitutional reform.

In a polity in which politicians are experience goods, recall that citizens do not actually discover the traits of their elected legislators until after the election. Personal and party reputations are relied upon as a sort of implicit guarantee that the legislator will live up to the expectations of the citizen-voter. When implicit, or self-enforcing, contracts are used to guarantee that agreements will be kept, there is the danger that parties will renege in the "last period." The last period problem arises in a political context because the value of an incumbent's name and reputation falls, once he decides to no longer seek reelection.[1] Unlike brandnames in private market transactions, political names and reputations are difficult to transfer to another owner. That is, while names like Campbell's or Del Monte can be bought and sold, there is not a viable market for an incumbent to capitalize on the value of his name reputation for political quality, once he decides to retire. Thus, when voters treat politicians as experience goods, the chances that legislators will not live up to the quality expectations of voters is high, and particularly so when the legislator is at the end of his career.[2] The longer the period as a lame duck, the more the legislator can "cheat" on voters by delivering political services that are lower than what he implicitly agreed to deliver.[3]

When legislators are treated as search goods by voters, the last period problem becomes a less important consideration than when the experience good analogy applies. Legislators are selected by voters based on direct information about particular political qualities, as opposed to implicit guarantees about the general quality of the service in the future. Reputations naturally become less valuable to voters in all elections when the search good analogy applies, that is, when reputations are not relied upon to guarantee quality as they are in the experience good setting. When legislators have been elected by voters who searched-out specific qualities, there is less reason to expect a problem to arise from lame ducks. Legislators who have been selected by voters based on actual qualities that both prefer are less likely to deviate. To change his position would mean that a legislator goes against his own preferences.

We expect the last period problem to be less important in democracy as voters adopt new shopping habits for candidates. This is exactly the interpretation we draw from the transformation of politics brought about by the implementation of legislative television.

Innovations in political information technology have reduced the role of reelection as a disciplinary mechanism. Of course, this is not to say that the disciplinary role of reelection is zero, but rather that it has become relatively less necessary as a means of maintaining citizen control over legislators. The changing nature of the reelection function due to modern technology is an important element in the consideration of constitutional forms. The impact of new technology on several constitutional choices are discussed below. In each case we describe the nature of the effect on the choice for particular values of the constitutional variable.

The first inference is that term lengths should not be as short as they were in times of pre-televised legislatures. There is less to fear from possible fallout from lame ducks serving out their final terms. Of course, the primary reason for having limited terms of office is to be able to oust a legislator who does not live up to citizen expectations. The new technology of telecommunications has lowered the likelihood that such disappointments will occur.[4]

A second constitutional issue concerns the sizes of legislatures. Chamber sizes could be smaller because telecommunications have made it easier for citizens to monitor the actions of their representatives. The desirable property of smaller chambers is that they would reduce the costs of reaching concensus among legislators. Several efforts to reform the U.S. Constitution have been motivated by a desire to "break the gridlock," which presumably means to economize on the resources being diverted to legislative decision-making.

The problem with moving to smaller legislatures is that they reduce the degree of representation that each citizen can expect from the process. What are the chances that a policy will be approved by the legislature that is not in an individual citizen's interest? Intuitively, these chances decline as the legislature gets larger; they rise as the legislature gets smaller (see Buchanan and Tullock, 1962).

Legislative television changes the basic ground rules under which legislative sizes were originally set. In selecting a particular size to reflect the relevant benefits and costs, some conditions were in mind about the ability of citizens to monitor their legislators. As technology alters these monitoring conditions making them less costly as in the case of legislative television, the direction for change is towards smaller legislatures.

A third constitutional variable that is affected is the number of expiration dates that are in effect. This variable determines the share of a legislative body that is elected at any one time. The Founding Fathers determined that while the length of the Senate term was to be six years, one third of the Senate would be elected every two years. The effects of term expiration dates on the control of politicians is not independent of the length of terms (See Crain and Shughart, 1987). Consider the polar case where the number of expiration dates is one; all members of the legislature are elected at the same time. How long does it take to turnover a majority of the legislature? When there is a single expiration date, it takes a period of time that is equivalent to the full term length. For a six-year term, it would require six years to replace a majority; for an eight-year term it would require eight years, and so on. Next, consider what happens when there are two expiration dates for a legislature. In the case of the six-year term, half of the legislature can be replaced in three years. In the eight-year legislature fifty percent can be tossed-out by the voters in four years. More expiration dates will shorten the length of time it takes voters to vote out a political majority, with which they might be dissatisfied.

By these simple examples we hope to illustrate that the political time horizon of a legislature is affected by the choice of the number of expiration dates that is selected. The Founding Fathers selected a value for the expiration date variable in order to place relatively narrow limits on how long "out-of-control" politicians could remain in power. How is this choice influenced by information technology? As politicians are transformed from experience to search goods, the need to cut short the average time required to replace a majority is reduced. Again, the reasoning is that the problems arising from lame ducks in their last electoral period will be diminished. Therefore, for any given term length, there could be fewer expiration dates, other things the same.

We could go on to analyze the choice of other particular pillars in the constitutional framework using this same reasoning. Also, other aspects of modern political life in America, such as political parties, can be treated with exactly the same analytical approach. We think it would only belabor the point, however, and we will close with a final thought about the prospects for constitutional reform.

The ability to take advantage of the opportunities to improve politics in America is justifiably feeble. If changes were easy, opportunities for abusing would be just as prevalent as opportunities for improving the democratic process. It is not our purpose here to take on the problem of a practical political strategy to implement the adjustments we have suggested. Our purpose has been to bring into focus new political relationships that have been created by information technology, and how technology changes the course of the process.

Footnotes

[1] This is precisely the point made by Lott in several articles, although Lott rejects the broader conceptual analogy that we employ throughout. Specifically, Lott argues that because politicians have always been susceptible to the last period problem, the "experience" product analogy is inappropriate. In other words, Lott sees politicians as analogous to search goods, always, but for different (and compelling) theoretical reasons. See Lott (1986a, 1986b, 1986c).

[2] For a relevant article on the transferability of political reputations, see Laband and Lentz (1985).

[3] This notion of "political cheating" is developed in Lott (1986b).

[4] Explanations of the term lengths set for national offices in the U.S. Constitution are contained in the *Federalist's Papers*. For two examples of economic and empirical analysis of term lengths, see Adams and Kenny (1986) and Crain and Tollison (1977).

Appendix 1

DATA SOURCES

Variables from *Book of the States 1976-1977* are:

(House) 1976 DISTRICT SIZE (p. 43),
(Senate) 1976 DISTRICT SIZE (p. 42),
(House) Multi Member Districts (p. 43),
(Senate) Multi Member Districts (p. 42),
SENATE TERM (p. 44),
COMPENSATION (p. 37),
RESTRICTIONS (p. 58-60).

Variables from *Book of the States 1977-1978* are:

(House) SEATS UP FOR ELECTION (p. 16),
(Senate) SEATS UP FOR ELECTION (p. 16),
(House) 1976 WINNING CHALLENGERS (p. 16),
(Senate) 1976 WINNING CHALLENGERS (p. 16),
SESSION LENGTH (p. 36-39),
BILLS PASSED (p. 36-39),
BILLS INTRODUCED (p. 36-39),
BICAMERALISM (House and Senate Sizes) (p. 16),
RECORDING METHOD (p. 36-39).

Variables from *Apportionment of State Legislatures* are:

(House) 1962 DISTRICT SIZE (p. A7-A8),
(Senate) 1962 DISTRICT SIZE (p. A7-A8).

Variables from *Book of the States 1966-1967* are:

> (House) 1962 SEATS UP FOR ELECTION (p. 43),
> (Senate) 1962 SEATS UP FOR ELECTION (p. 43).

Variables from *State Legislatures in American Politics* are:

> (House) 1962 WINNING CHALLENGERS (p. 104),
> (Senate) 1962 WINNING CHALLENGERS (p. 104).

Variables from *America Votes* are:

> VOTE78, VOTE80, and DREP (various pages).

Variables from *FEC Reports on Financial Activity 1977-1978* are:

> OEXP78 and OEXP80 (various pages).

Variables from *Almanac of American Politics, 1984* are:

> TENURE, LVOTE, and D86 (various pages).

Variables from *Congressional Quarterly Almanac, 1984 ,* are:

> VOTE and DDEM (p. 41-45), D86 (various pages).

(U.S. House) DED is from *Congressional Districts in the 1970's.*

(U.S. Senate) DED is from *Congressional Districts in the 1980's.*

Appendix 2

DATA

The data listed below are for U.S. state houses and are used in Chapters 2 and 5. The data are listed by state in alphabetical order from Alabama to Wyoming. Alabama, Maryland, and Nebraska are not used in the regressions in those chapters for reasons noted in the text.

State Houses

	Winning Challengers (1976)	District Size (1976)	Multi-Member Districts (1976)
AL	0.00000	62802.0	0.00000
AK	18.0000	7559.00	10.0000
AZ	17.0000	29541.0	30.0000
AR	20.0000	19233.0	10.0000
CA	20.0000	249661.	0.00000
CO	17.0000	33993.0	0.00000
CT	57.0000	20081.0	0.00000
DE	10.0000	13368.0	0.00000
FL	33.0000	56591.0	24.0000
GA	46.0000	25502.0	17.0000
HI	14.0000	6624.00	22.0000
ID	25.0000	10186.0	35.0000
IL	46.0000	62791.0	59.0000
IN	26.0000	51936.0	20.0000
IA	19.0000	28253.0	0.00000
KN	48.0000	18223.0	0.00000
KY	25.0000	32193.0	0.00000
LA	33.0000	34697.0	0.00000

	Winning Challengers (1976)	District Size (1976)	Multi- Member Districts (1976)
ME	55.0000	6581.00	11.0000
MD	0.00000	27818.0	47.0000
MA	57.0000	23232.0	0.00000
MI	15.0000	80751.0	0.00000
MN	30.0000	28404.0	0.00000
MS	52.0000	18171.0	27.0000
MO	44.0000	28696.0	0.00000
MT	41.0000	6944.00	0.00000
NE	0.00000	0.00000	0.00000
NV	10.0000	12218.0	0.00000
NH	175.000	1813.00	109.000
NJ	23.0000	89639.0	40.0000
NM	21.0000	14514.0	0.00000
NY	31.0000	121608.	0.00000
NL	30.0000	42350.0	35.0000
ND	35.0000	6178.00	49.0000
OH	15.0000	107596.	0.00000
OK	15.0000	25338.0	0.00000
OR	17.0000	34856.0	0.00000
PA	52.0000	58115.0	0.00000
RI	37.0000	8900.00	0.00000
SL	35.0000	20819.0	0.00000
SD	28.0000	9518.00	28.0000
TN	27.0000	39638.0	0.00000
TX	47.0000	74645.0	0.00000
UT	25.0000	14124.0	0.00000
VT	52.0000	1820.00	39.0000
VA	18.0000	46485.0	28.0000
WA	35.0000	34214.0	49.0000
WV	38.0000	17442.0	25.0000
WI	24.0000	44626.0	0.00000
WY	22.0000	5362.00	12.0000

	Seats Up (1976)	Winning Challengers (1962)	District Size (1962)
AL	105.000	63.0000	30818.0
AK	40.0000	17.0000	5654.00
AZ	60.0000	35.0000	16277.0
AR	100.000	29.0000	17863.0
CA	80.0000	39.0000	196465.
CO	65.0000	23.0000	26984.0
CT	151.000	105.000	8623.00
DE	41.0000	14.0000	12751.0
FL	120.000	29.0000	52122.0
GA	180.000	84.0000	19235.0
HI	51.0000	13.0000	12407.0
ID	70.0000	23.0000	10590.0
IL	177.000	38.0000	170865.
IN	100.000	41.0000	46625.0
IA	100.000	24.0000	25532.0
KN	125.000	34.0000	17428.0
KY	100.000	67.0000	30382.0
LA	105.000	5.00000	31019.0
ME	151.000	78.0000	6418.00
MD	141.000	81.0000	29290.0
MA	240.000	55.0000	21452.0
MI	110.000	24.0000	71120.0
MN	134.000	57.0000	26060.0
MS	122.000	7.00000	15558.0
MD	163.000	61.0000	26502.0
MT	100.000	42.0000	7178.00
NE	49.0000	0.00000	0.00000
NV	40.0000	12.0000	7710.00
NH	400.000	155.000	1517.00
NJ	80.0000	26.0000	10113.0
NM	70.0000	28.0000	14394.0
NY	150.000	27.0000	111882.
NC	120.000	52.0000	37968.0
ND	102.000	38.0000	5499.00

	Seats Up (1976)	Winning Challengers (1962)	District Size 1962)
OH	99.0000	35.0000	70850.0
OK	101.000	42.0000	19242.0
OR	60.0000	25.0000	29478.0
PA	203.000	46.0000	53902.0
RI	100.000	30.0000	8594.00
SC	124.000	47.0000	19214.0
SD	70.0000	30.0000	9074.00
TN	99.0000	57.0000	36031.0
TX	150.000	67.0000	62864.0
UT	75.0000	39.0000	13916.0
VT	150.000	98.0000	1585.00
VA	100.000	21.0000	39669.0
WA	98.0000	26.0000	28820.0
WV	100.000	44.0000	18604.0
WI	99.0000	21.0000	39528.0
WY	62.0000	15.0000	5894.00

	Seats Up (1962)
AL	106.000
AK	40.0000
AZ	80.0000
AR	100.000
CA	80.0000
CO	65.0000
CT	294.000
DE	35.0000
FL	95.0000
GA	205.000
HI	51.0000
ID	59.0000
IL	177.000

	Seats Up (1962)
IN	100.000
IA	108.000
KN	125.000
KY	100.000
LA	105.000
ME	151.000
MD	123.000
MA	240.000
MI	110.000
MN	135.000
MS	140.000
MO	157.000
MT	94.0000
ME	0.00000
NV	47.0000
NH	400.000
NJ	60.0000
NM	66.0000
NY	150.000
NC	120.000
ND	115.000
OH	139.000
OK	121.000
OR	60.0000
PA	210.000
RI	100.000
SC	124.000
SD	75.0000
TN	99.0000
TX	150.000
UT	64.0000
VT	246.000
VA	100.000
WA	99.0000
WV	100.000
WI	100.000
WY	56.0000

The data listed below are for U.S. state senates and are used in Chapters 2 and 5. Alabama, Maryland, and Nebraska are not used in the regressions in those chapters for reasons cited in the text.

State Senates

	Winning Challengers (1976)	District Size (1976)	Multi-Member Districts (1976)
AL	0.00000	98406.0	0.00000
AK	2.00000	15118.0	3.00000
AZ	11.0000	59083.0	0.00000
AR	3.00000	54923.0	0.00000
CA	13.0000	499322.	0.00000
CO	8.00000	63129.0	0.00000
CT	12.0000	84228.0	0.00000
DE	5.00000	26100.0	0.00000
FL	6.00000	169773.	14.0000
GA	9.00000	81955.0	0.00000
HI	0.00000	13513.0	7.00000
ID	8.00000	20371.0	0.00000
IL	17.0000	188372.	0.00000
IN	17.0000	103872.	0.00000
IA	13.0000	56507.0	0.00000
KN	15.0000	86321.0	0.00000
KY	7.00000	84791.0	0.00000
LA	16.0000	93415.0	0.00000
ME	16.0000	30111.0	0.00000
MD	0.00000	83455.0	0.00000
MA	5.00000	138493.	0.00000
MI	0.00000	233753.	0.00000
MN	21.0000	56870.0	0.00000
MS	16.0000	42000.0	12.0000
MO	13.0000	137571.	0.00000
MT	10.0000	13888.0	0.00000
NE	15.0000	30280.0	0.00000

	Winning Challengers (1976)	District Size (1976)	Multi-Member Districts (1976)
NV	4.00000	24437.0	3.00000
NH	3.00000	30154.0	0.00000
NJ	18.0000	179278.	0.00000
NM	15.0000	24190.0	0.00000
NY	7.00000	304021.	0.00000
NC	17.0000	101641.	18.0000
ND	16.0000	12355.0	1.00000
OH	10.0000	322788.	0.00000
OK	8.00000	53317.0	0.00000
OR	3.00000	69713.0	0.00000
PA	7.00000	235949.	0.00000
RI	13.0000	17800.0	0.00000
SC	18.0000	56316.0	13.0000
SD	13.0000	19035.0	3.00000
TN	8.00000	118914.	0.00000
TX	5.00000	361185.	0.00000
UT	9.00000	36527.0	0.00000
VT	8.00000	14824.0	11.0000
VA	0.00000	116212.	1.00000
WA	6.00000	68428.0	0.00000
WV	5.00000	54718.0	17.0000
WI	11.0000	133877.	0.00000
WY	9.00000	11080.0	9.00000

	Seats Up (1976)	Winning Challengers (1962)	Seats Up (1962)
AL	35.0000	28.0000	35.0000
AK	10.0000	7.00000	10.0000
AZ	30.0000	7.00000	28.0000
AR	17.0000	13.0000	17.0000

	Seats Up (1976)	Winning Challengers (1962)	Seats Up (1962)
CA	20.0000	11.0000	20.0000
CO	17.0000	7.00000	17.0000
CT	36.0000	10.0000	36.0000
DE	10.0000	4.00000	8.00000
FL	20.0000	10.0000	19.0000
GA	56.0000	48.0000	54.0000
HI	25.0000	10.0000	12.0000
ID	35.0000	15.0000	44.0000
IL	20.0000	11.0000	29.0000
IN	25.0000	13.0000	25.0000
IA	25.0000	16.0000	25.0000
KN	40.0000	5.00000	40.0000
KY	19.0000	13.0000	19.0000
LA	19.0000	4.00000	19.0000
ME	33.0000	13.0000	33.0000
MD	47.0000	14.0000	29.0000
MA	40.0000	12.0000	40.0000
MI	38.0000	11.0000	34.0000
MN	67.0000	23.0000	67.0000
MS	52.0000	2.00000	49.0000
NO	17.0000	6.00000	16.0000
MT	25.0000	11.0000	28.0000
NE	24.0000	15.0000	43.0000
NV	10.0000	5.00000	8.00000
NH	24.0000	13.0000	24.0000
NJ	40.0000	3.00000	10.0000
NM	42.0000	0.00000	0.00000
NY	60.0000	9.00000	58.0000
NC	50.0000	33.0000	50.0000
ND	25.0000	14.0000	24.0000
OH	16.0000	9.00000	16.0000
OK	24.0000	10.0000	22.0000
OR	15.0000	10.0000	15.0000
PA	25.0000	11.0000	25.0000
RI	50.0000	18.0000	46.0000

	Seats Up (1976)	Winning Challengers (1962)	Seats Up (1962)
SC	46.0000	12.0000	23.0000
SD	35.0000	14.0000	35.0000
TN	16.0000	18.0000	33.0000
TX	15.0000	12.0000	31.0000
UT	14.0000	9.00000	12.0000
VT	30.0000	11.0000	30.0000
VA	40.0000	2.00000	40.0000
WA	24.0000	9.00000	24.0000
WV	17.0000	6.00000	16.0000
WI	16.0000	8.00000	16.0000
WY	15.0000	7.00000	13.0000

	District Size (1962)
AL	93278.0
AK	11308.0
AZ	46506.0
AR	51036.0
CA	392930.
CO	50113.0
CT	70423.0
DE	26193.0
FL	130304.
GA	73021.0
HI	25311.0
ID	15163.0
IL	173812.
IN	93250.0
IA	55100.0
KN	54465.0
KY	79951.0

	District Size (1962)
LA	83513.0
ME	28508.0
MD	106920.
MA	128174.
MI	200682.
MN	50953.0
MS	44452.0
MO	127053.
MT	12049.0
NC	32822.0
NV	16781.0
NH	25288.0
NJ	288894.
NM	29719.0
NY	287626.
NC	91123.0
ND	12907.0
OH	288073.
OK	52916.0
OR	58956.0
PA	226387.
RI	18684.0
SC	51796.0
SD	19443.0
TN	108093.
TX	309022.
UT	35625.0
VT	12996.0
VA	99174.0
WA	58229.0
WV	58138.0
WI	119780.
WY	12225.0

The data listed below are for U.S. legislatures and are used in the fifth chapter. Alabama, Maryland, and Nebraska are not use in the regressions in that chapter for reasons mentioned in the text.

State Legislatures

	Bills Passed	Bills Introduced	Senate Term
AL	1476.00	5289.00	1.00000
AK	440.000	1696.00	1.00000
AZ	355.000	1748.00	0.00000
AR	1238.00	2098.00	1.00000
CA	2767.00	6747.00	1.00000
CO	546.000	1369.00	1.00000
CT	1232.00	7478.00	0.00000
DE	722.000	2185.00	1.00000
FL	1077.00	7551.00	1.00000
GA	1465.00	2812.00	0.00000
HI	441.000	6476.00	1.00000
ID	637.000	1301.00	0.00000
IL	1364.00	6080.00	1.00000
IN	410.000	2658.00	1.00000
IA	517.000	2443.00	1.00000
KN	949.000	2322.00	1.00000
KY	368.000	1245.00	1.00000
LA	769.000	5114.00	1.00000
ME	733.000	1823.00	0.00000
MD	1823.00	6218.00	1.00000
MA	1445.00	16260.0	0.00000
MI	790.000	4402.00	1.00000
MN	785.000	5397.00	1.00000
MS	1308.00	5172.00	1.00000
MO	279.000	2734.00	1.00000
MT	572.000	1124.00	1.00000
NE	522.000	1011.00	0.00000
NV	768.000	1426.00	1.00000
NH	507.000	1371.00	0.00000
NJ	610.000	4353.00	1.00000

	Bills Passed	Bills Introduced	Senate Term
NM	444.000	1383.00	1.00000
NY	1861.00	3393.00	0.00000
NC	983.000	2311.00	0.00000
ND	597.000	1112.00	1.00000
OH	447.000	1180.00	1.00000
OK	619.000	1794.00	1.00000
OR	795.000	2449.00	1.00000
PA	570.000	4416.00	1.00000
RI	1311.00	4711.00	0.00000
SC	922.000	2480.00	1.00000
SD	683.000	1337.00	0.00000
TN	1148.00	4855.00	1.00000
TX	762.000	3375.00	1.00000
UT	258.000	875.000	1.00000
VT	254.000	773.000	0.00000
VA	1541.00	3478.00	1.00000
WA	518.000	2949.00	1.00000
WV	361.000	3221.00	1.00000
WI	414.000	2325.00	1.00000
WY	237.000	821.000	1.00000

	Bicameralism	State Employees	Sessions Length
AL	.333333	17889.5	74.0000
AK	.500000	38743.5	281.000
AZ	.500000	17871.8	317.000
AR	.350000	17484.1	93.0000
CA	.500000	12826.6	256.000
CO	.538462	20857.9	318.000
CT	.238411	15063.2	152.000
DE	.512195	25690.7	111.000
FL	.333333	12859.5	119.000
GA	.311111	17033.2	85.0000

	Bicameralism	State Employees	Session Length
HI	.490196	47570.5	120.000
ID	.500000	22530.7	144.000
IL	.333333	12417.3	188.000
IN	.500000	15257.8	91.0000
IA	.500000	16795.5	199.000
KN	.320000	20413.4	140.000
KY	.380000	18682.0	60.0000
LA	.371429	20896.4	120.000
ME	.218543	19492.5	109.000
MD	.333333	17641.7	180.000
MA	.166667	13196.2	319.000
MI	.345455	15331.2	166.000
MN	.500000	16981.1	106.000
MS	.426230	16763.3	215.000
MO	.208589	15219.3	159.000
MT	.500000	25573.7	86.0000
NE	0.00000	19324.5	151.000
NV	.500000	18373.8	83.0000
NH	.600000E-01	20535.3	70.0000
NJ	.500000	11146.7	72.0000
NM	.600000	26369.9	90.0000
NY	.400000	10658.2	392.000
NC	.416667	17601.9	127.000
ND	.500000	24990.7	57.0000
OH	.333333	11988.1	183.000
OK	.475248	21175.0	178.000
OR	.500000	22149.4	153.000
PA	.246305	12383.6	143.000
RI	.500000	24195.3	151.000
SC	.370968	20353.2	206.000
SD	.500000	23154.5	75.0000
TN	.333333	16356.0	91.0000
TX	.206667	14837.0	140.000
UT	.386667	24505.7	80.0000
VT	.200000	26413.9	113.000
VA	.400000	1840.25	112.000

	Bicameralism	State Employees	Session Length
WA	.500000	26532.3	60.0000
WF	.340000	23114.8	219.000
WI	.333333	16543.7	125.000
WY	.483871	24171.8	60.0000

	Compensation	Restrictions	Recording Method
AL	12940.0	1.00000	0.00000
AK	43000.0	0.00000	0.00000
AZ	19170.0	0.00000	1.00000
AR	3600.00	1.00000	1.00000
CA	64140.0	0.00000	0.00000
CO	15200.0	0.00000	1.00000
CT	13000.0	1.00000	0.00000
DE	21050.0	1.00000	0.00000
FL	27125.0	1.00000	1.00000
GA	18432.0	1.00000	0.00000
HI	27000.0	1.00000	0.00000
ID	7535.00	1.00000	1.00000
IL	49424.0	0.00000	0.00000
IN	21420.0	1.00000	0.00000
IA	21580.0	0.00000	0.00000
KN	18928.0	1.00000	0.00000
KY	12350.0	1.00000	0.00000
LA	18000.0	1.00000	0.00000
ME	4250.00	0.00000	0.00000
MD	25000.0	1.00000	1.00000
MA	27776.0	0.00000	0.00000
MI	38000.0	0.00000	0.00000
MN	23862.0	1.00000	0.00000
MS	26480.0	1.00000	1.00000
MO	16800.0	1.00000	0.00000
MT	6954.00	1.00000	0.00000

	Compensation	Restrictions	Recording Method
NE	10000.0	1.00000	0.00000
NV	8260.00	1.00000	0.00000
NH	200.000	1.00000	0.00000
NJ	20000.0	0.00000	0.00000
NM	3600.00	1.00000	1.00000
NY	56500.0	0.00000	1.00000
NC	17635.0	0.00000	0.00000
ND	6540.00	1.00000	0.00000
OH	35000.0	0.00000	0.00000
OK	19920.0	1.00000	0.00000
OR	20010.0	0.00000	1.00000
PA	31200.0	0.00000	0.00000
RI	600.000	1.00000	0.00000
SC	14400.0	0.00000	0.00000
SD	7475.00	1.00000	0.00000
TN	19909.0	1.00000	1.00000
TX	17400.0	1.00000	1.00000
UT	3200.00	1.00000	1.00000
VT	8430.00	0.00000	0.00000
VA	25850.0	1.00000	1.00000
WA	11200.0	1.00000	1.00000
WV	12600.0	1.00000	1.00000
WI	31356.0	0.00000	0.00000
WY	3348.00	1.00000	0.00000

The following data for U.S. House races are used in Chapter 4. The data are listed in aphabetical order from Alabama (1st District) thru Wyoming. The following districts are ommitted because the incumbent did not run for reelection in 1980: AL (6); CA (11,31,41); CO (4); CT (2,3); FL (5,12); GA (2); ID (1); IL (1,2,10,16); IN (4); IA (3); KA (1); KY (5); LA (3); MA (4); MI (13,14); MN (6); MO (8); NE (2); NH (2); NJ (15); NM (2); NY (5,16,30,32); ND; OH (6,22); OK (4); OR (3); PA (1,11,14); SC (1); SD (2); TX (4,14); VA (3); WV (2,3); and WI (6).

	VOTE80	VOTE78	DED
1	94.8000	63.9000	86.4000
2	60.6000	54.0000	83.2000
3	100.000	100.000	86.2000
4	97.9000	100.000	91.8000
5	94.1000	96.8000	78.2000
6	72.6000	93.8000	85.2000
7	73.8000	55.4000	71.8000
8	73.3000	71.0000	76.2000
9	58.1000	52.5000	70.8000
10	64.3000	85.0000	80.6000
11	62.6000	63.1000	72.0000
12	100.000	100.000	90.2000
13	78.9000	51.2000	82.0000
14	100.000	78.4000	86.8000
15	100.000	100.000	88.2000
16	39.8000	59.4000	79.2000
17	54.2000	52.0000	81.0000
18	70.6000	53.4000	72.4000
19	65.1000	55.4000	76.6000
20	51.1000	66.8000	72.2000
21	69.4000	68.3000	53.2000
22	63.3000	63.4000	52.4000
23	55.5000	57.4000	78.4000
24	55.3000	65.4000	82.0000
25	62.1000	67.1000	53.4000
26	72.2000	73.1000	72.8000
27	58.9000	57.5000	69.4000
28	60.7000	53.4000	71.4000
29	71.8000	60.1000	84.6000
30	71.0000	61.4000	80.4000
31	70.6000	54.5000	52.0000
32	71.0000	59.2000	84.0000
33	77.7000	71.7000	88.0000
34	78.8000	66.4000	63.4000
35	48.2000	59.5000	92.2000
36	63.9000	64.6000	81.8000
37	63.2000	65.6000	77.2000

	VOTE80	VOTE78	DED
38	63.8000	62.7000	72.4000
39	66.0000	67.4000	74.6000
40	70.9000	100.000	62.2000
41	51.0000	51.0000	62.6000
42	79.2000	100.000	45.4000
43	86.1000	85.0000	82.4000
44	72.1000	71.4000	82.4000
45	65.9000	71.4000	68.6000
46	70.9000	56.0000	70.8000
47	71.8000	53.7000	85.0000
48	45.4000	54.0000	85.0000
49	52.5000	62.9000	78.8000
50	71.6000	61.4000	78.2000
51	55.5000	58.6000	89.2000
52	76.3000	63.7000	62.4000
53	70.2000	65.9000	58.4000
54	46.7000	73.7000	66.8000
55	86.5000	68.7000	78.4000
56	59.8000	61.5000	65.2000
57	56.4000	52.9000	61.6000
58	54.9000	49.3000	82.6000
59	72.4000	59.8000	67.4000
60	63.0000	59.5000	72.8000
61	62.6000	58.4000	65.6000
62	50.4000	52.3000	72.8000
63	59.0000	64.2000	75.4000
64	61.8000	58.2000	73.8000
65	61.2000	63.3000	81.0000
66	70.6000	81.7000	74.0000
67	77.0000	100.000	84.6000
68	65.8000	73.1000	79.8000
69	100.000	78.8000	80.0000
70	71.8000	100.000	82.2000
71	69.3000	100.000	80.0000
72	70.4000	61.5000	71.6000
73	78.9000	100.000	80.2000
74	59.5000	55.3000	77.4000

	VOTE80	VOTE78	DED
75	74.9000	100.000	84.2000
76	74.9000	63.1000	80.8000
77	65.4000	74.2000	71.0000
78	100.000	100.000	85.0000
79	100.000	100.000	83.2000
80	64.9000	80.9000	64.6000
81	74.0000	75.5000	67.0000
82	59.1000	54.4000	86.4000
83	68.1000	66.5000	86.4000
84	74.6000	100.000	87.2000
85	68.0000	76.9000	89.6000
86	80.2000	100.000	80.2000
87	79.8000	73.3000	65.6000
88	89.9000	85.7000	78.4000
89	58.8000	57.3000	79.4000
90	68.9000	65.2000	84.8000
91	68.0000	66.9000	74.0000
92	79.6000	84.0000	93.2000
93	67.0000	66.2000	79.2000
94	85.1000	86.3000	88.6000
95	84.7000	86.0000	90.8000
96	73.1000	75.3000	66.8000
97	69.8000	73.7000	86.2000
98	74.1000	79.5000	55.4000
99	71.7000	61.2000	78.0000
100	76.8000	75.1000	58.4000
101	76.7000	62.4000	82.6000
102	65.8000	70.6000	85.0000
103	62.1000	65.9000	82.8000
104	73.4000	100.000	85.0000
105	56.0000	69.6000	84.2000
106	67.6000	78.3000	70.6000
107	68.8000	54.0000	88.2000
108	64.4000	74.2000	86.8000
109	49.1000	65.6000	88.0000
110	72.0000	80.3000	88.0000
111	54.1000	56.5000	79.0000

	VOTE80	VOTE78	DED
112	45.0000	55.5000	82.6000
113	61.7000	67.6000	80.4000
114	50.2000	52.2000	86.0000
115	66.1000	56.3000	80.4000
116	55.2000	52.0000	86.8000
117	64.4000	65.6000	88.4000
118	53.4000	56.1000	86.2000
119	57.3000	57.2000	75.8000
120	64.1000	63.5000	76.6000
121	54.0000	52.3000	82.0000
122	53.9000	64.7000	79.8000
123	60.2000	58.9000	83.0000
124	64.3000	66.3000	84.4000
125	53.9000	52.0000	76.8000
126	55.5000	100.000	65.6000
127	68.9000	69.5000	76.0000
128	74.2000	57.0000	84.6000
129	100.000	100.000	89.6000
130	65.7000	100.000	86.8000
131	63.7000	65.7000	84.6000
132	67.0000	65.8000	79.2000
133	58.9000	50.6000	78.8000
134	100.000	76.5000	90.2000
135	88.0000	86.0000	80.6000
136	61.0000	87.0000	81.0000
137	36.0000	50.1000	81.4000
138	89.0000	52.0000	84.0000
139	91.0000	91.0000	74.8000
140	100.000	60.0000	83.6000
141	69.0000	80.0000	88.8000
142	68.5000	61.5000	80.8000
143	78.5000	50.8000	85.8000
144	48.3000	63.5000	83.2000
145	57.4000	66.4000	73.8000
146	76.1000	100.000	83.6000
147	71.9000	62.0000	72.8000
148	80.5000	77.2000	63.8000

	VOTE80	VOTE78	DED
149	69.9000	89.7000	80.6000
150	88.5000	88.7000	87.0000
151	59.3000	51.3000	31.8000
152	74.9000	99.9000	77.0000
153	67.2000	72.8000	82.4000
154	73.2000	75.2000	80.0000
155	66.0000	52.2000	72.4000
156	50.8000	53.8000	76.4000
157	100.000	84.8000	78.6000
158	78.4000	74.6000	63.6000
159	100.000	91.8000	74.6000
160	60.6000	61.1000	77.2000
161	100.000	91.7000	82.2000
162	73.2000	99.9000	76.8000
163	94.7000	92.9000	84.4000
164	57.3000	67.6000	62.2000
165	52.0000	51.3000	78.2000
166	74.7000	70.6000	85.0000
167	53.1000	49.4000	81.0000
168	49.4000	56.7000	73.2000
169	92.7000	76.6000	85.4000
170	60.7000	66.6000	87.2000
171	96.5000	69.6000	86.0000
172	52.4000	51.5000	81.8000
173	65.5000	54.9000	85.8000
174	55.3000	54.9000	85.2000
175	67.6000	79.6000	86.8000
176	69.9000	76.5000	86.4000
177	73.1000	95.2000	74.4000
178	65.3000	74.5000	75.2000
179	72.7000	71.3000	67.6000
180	71.8000	56.2000	77.6000
181	60.6000	70.4000	80.0000
182	76.6000	65.7000	61.8000
183	58.5000	58.0000	71.6000
184	70.1000	62.3000	74.4000
185	52.1000	52.4000	86.6000

	VOTE80	VOTE78	DED
186	70.4000	87.2000	83.8000
187	63.0000	66.6000	87.0000
188	69.6000	61.7000	84.2000
189	100.000	92.3000	88.4000
190	39.0000	51.6000	77.2000
191	73.9000	100.000	82.6000
192	70.2000	66.6000	80.6000
193	64.4000	56.4000	65.4000
194	77.6000	81.9000	85.0000
195	67.8000	72.8000	85.0000
196	70.1000	72.0000	80.0000
197	70.6000	55.9000	84.6000
198	67.8000	61.2000	86.6000
199	56.5000	74.7000	84.2000
200	44.8000	65.3000	89.8000
201	61.4000	57.3000	76.2000
202	59.1000	56.9000	79.8000
203	78.6000	58.1000	80.4000
204	83.9000	80.0000	86.0000
205	67.5000	69.5000	78.4000
206	60.8000	61.6000	79.0000
207	76.7000	79.4000	86.0000
208	57.5000	66.4000	87.8000
209	49.9000	56.0000	72.6000
210	40.6000	61.1000	79.6000
211	77.5000	72.6000	51.0000
212	56.3000	60.4000	73.4000
213	46.5000	52.5000	64.0000
214	67.2000	74.5000	84.2000
215	59.1000	48.9000	75.6000
216	85.3000	86.4000	87.8000
217	63.0000	70.5000	70.8000
218	77.1000	73.4000	69.6000
219	71.6000	51.8000	74.8000
220	64.2000	63.6000	88.6000
221	51.0000	62.5000	69.4000
222	56.3000	56.3000	74.2000

	VOTE80	VOTE78	DED
223	56.3000	54.9000	83.8000
224	47.5000	50.9000	64.8000
225	66.8000	66.1000	69.8000
226	47.2000	60.0000	63.4000
227	95.3000	94.9000	79.0000
228	75.6000	78.6000	72.0000
229	58.3000	54.2000	87.8000
230	94.5000	95.0000	89.0000
231	74.1000	78.5000	85.8000
232	87.1000	87.8000	93.8000
233	79.4000	81.1000	84.8000
234	76.1000	76.9000	88.0000
235	50.2000	68.1000	86.2000
236	35.0000	54.2000	77.2000
237	56.7000	53.3000	32.8000
238	96.2000	96.4000	79.6000
239	82.4000	84.6000	62.2000
240	98.2000	98.0000	96.2000
241	83.9000	84.1000	85.8000
242	56.2000	51.6000	67.4000
243	59.4000	56.1000	57.2000
244	81.0000	78.2000	70.8000
245	74.3000	62.3000	72.0000
246	55.0000	55.8000	74.0000
247	77.9000	76.3000	73.2000
248	66.7000	54.0000	81.0000
249	77.5000	100.000	83.4000
250	75.8000	56.0000	79.6000
251	72.9000	87.1000	68.2000
252	72.2000	69.4000	80.6000
253	71.7000	74.1000	80.4000
254	83.0000	78.6000	87.4000
255	81.6000	94.8000	74.0000
256	54.7000	58.5000	82.4000
257	100.000	80.1000	86.2000
258	73.4000	78.2000	83.0000
259	68.3000	71.1000	88.4000

	VOTE80	VOTE78	DED
260	52.6000	94.4000	72.4000
261	51.0000	54.2000	84.4000
262	48.9000	68.4000	79.0000
263	68.7000	69.9000	83.8000
264	58.5000	59.0000	88.8000
265	58.6000	68.3000	76.2000
266	69.7000	100.000	87.2000
267	46.5000	53.4000	85.2000
268	74.7000	65.0000	71.6000
269	58.7000	52.0000	77.6000
270	57.3000	54.0000	75.8000
271	72.3000	68.0000	86.4000
272	70.4000	63.0000	86.2000
273	76.1000	100.000	82.2000
274	76.0000	71.0000	85.4000
275	39.9000	68.0000	81.0000
276	74.4000	74.0000	87.6000
277	69.3000	68.0000	81.6000
278	47.4000	57.0000	77.0000
279	63.8000	65.0000	85.2000
280	64.9000	72.0000	78.4000
281	72.6000	71.0000	67.8000
282	79.3000	78.0000	85.2000
283	72.9000	67.0000	86.4000
284	76.1000	60.0000	91.0000
285	58.1000	51.0000	85.6000
286	100.000	100.000	92.4000
287	88.2000	86.0000	88.4000
288	100.000	75.0000	70.4000
289	58.4000	59.9000	75.2000
290	54.0000	54.8000	85.2000
291	100.000	100.000	87.6000
292	68.4000	79.9000	73.2000
293	64.7000	74.2000	78.4000
294	65.9000	62.9000	65.0000
295	47.5000	69.1000	80.6000
296	54.8000	56.3000	79.4000

	VOTE80	VOTE78	DED
297	96.4000	82.0000	78.4000
298	54.5000	71.8000	90.6000
299	63.3000	55.8000	87.4000
300	75.1000	75.1000	65.6000
301	67.1000	73.8000	89.2000
302	53.1000	50.3000	77.2000
303	48.7000	61.1000	74.6000
304	100.000	74.9000	89.0000
305	76.6000	76.5000	87.0000
306	59.4000	68.7000	89.2000
307	70.0000	70.9000	61.2000
308	59.5000	53.2000	83.2000
309	76.9000	77.0000	84.2000
310	60.6000	59.6000	85.4000
311	68.5000	57.1000	74.4000
312	70.6000	78.7000	82.4000
313	72.5000	72.1000	83.4000
314	68.4000	52.9000	83.8000
315	69.6000	71.6000	85.8000
316	73.5000	54.3000	82.2000
317	49.7000	64.0000	83.4000
318	67.1000	46.5000	86.4000
319	67.6000	61.2000	79.6000
320	44.7000	52.6000	82.8000
321	55.7000	57.3000	74.8000
322	59.8000	82.0000	84.2000
323	92.6000	52.1000	81.0000
324	87.5000	82.7000	85.4000
325	48.2000	100.000	86.0000
326	68.5000	50.1000	81.8000
327	100.000	64.5000	86.8000
328	76.1000	81.8000	82.8000
329	61.1000	88.9000	82.2000
330	79.3000	100.000	88.4000
331	65.4000	51.4000	77.2000
332	99.6000	74.6000	84.8000
333	77.3000	72.9000	88.6000

	VOTE80	VOTE78	DED
334	99.9000	69.7000	82.8000
335	100.000	78.1000	87.6000
336	69.3000	70.1000	85.8000
337	79.3000	100.000	53.6000
338	51.0000	50.3000	77.4000
339	70.9000	65.1000	74.4000
340	82.1000	85.1000	42.2000
341	48.2000	61.5000	88.2000
342	99.7000	63.3000	81.4000
343	59.1000	76.3000	71.0000
344	100.000	51.6000	83.2000
345	59.9000	68.5000	83.2000
346	55.0000	74.9000	80.6000
347	70.0000	66.2000	85.0000
348	84.6000	70.0000	79.0000
349	100.000	68.1000	84.4000
350	79.9000	96.8000	85.2000
351	93.5000	53.2000	76.0000
352	81.9000	100.000	88.8000
353	76.5000	57.0000	72.0000
354	51.0000	50.6000	71.0000
355	69.8000	89.7000	86.8000
356	61.3000	54.1000	78.4000
357	47.9000	51.0000	73.0000
358	67.0000	62.3000	71.0000
359	79.2000	75.3000	77.0000
360	90.5000	72.1000	80.0000
361	89.8000	100.000	77.8000
362	60.7000	99.9000	87.2000
363	99.9000	99.9000	88.2000
364	99.2000	99.8000	81.6000
365	99.7000	64.3000	81.4000
366	48.3000	50.5000	51.0000
367	69.4000	61.9000	88.8000
368	48.9000	53.3000	42.8000
369	78.3000	64.0000	57.6000
370	63.9000	51.4000	77.8000

	VOTE80	VOTE78	DED
371	62.7000	58.6000	81.8000
372	42.6000	61.1000	79.6000
373	51.9000	48.0000	76.2000
374	53.6000	60.9000	78.6000
375	57.3000	53.3000	71.4000
376	63.6000	63.4000	86.2000
377	76.6000	100.000	87.8000
378	56.2000	54.5000	82.4000
379	54.0000	57.7000	68.4000
380	49.0000	62.8000	83.4000
381	70.0000	66.1000	82.6000
382	77.0000	73.1000	83.0000
383	64.7000	62.2000	85.8000
384	67.7000	57.9000	85.0000
385	78.4000	61.1000	68.0000
386	68.6000	58.6000	76.4000

	OEXP80	OEXP78	DREP
1	0.00000	.340060	1.00000
2	.193498	.452999	1.00000
3	0.00000	0.00000	0.00000
4	0.00000	0.00000	0.00000
5	0.00000	0.00000	0.00000
6	0.00000	.863971E-01	1.00000
7	.164950	.3556281	.00000
8	0.00000	.303929E-01	1.00000
9	.462447	.312673	0.00000
10	.304975E-01	0.00000	0.00000
11	.401418	.116758	1.00000
12	0.00000	0.00000	0.00000
13	.716825E-01	.563702	1.00000
14	0.00000	0.00000	1.00000
15	0.00000	0.00000	0.00000
16	.497983	.287903	1.00000

	OEXP80	OEXP78	DREP
17	.297141	.285885	1.00000
18	0.00000	.413084	0.00000
19	.289125E-01	.369522	0.00000
20	.567323	0.00000	0.00000
21	.467512E-01	0.00000	0.00000
22	.224877	.469080	0.00000
23	.209058	.945778E-01	0.00000
24	.314095	.226551	0.00000
25	.502395E-01	.441826	0.00000
26	.769661E-01	.481813	1.00000
27	.408631E-01	.236596	0.00000
28	.217670	.487975	1.00000
29	.352946E-01	.281328	0.00000
30	.178577	.456399	0.00000
31	.132498	.375935	1.00000
32	.642152E-01	.460730	1.00000
33	0.00000	.128724	1.00000
34	.739629E-01	.652502	1.00000
35	.382400	.952925E-01	1.00000
36	.580466	.191686	1.00000
37	.138828	.161030	0.00000
38	.203741	.650372	0.00000
39	.249332	0.00000	0.00000
40	.306797	0.00000	1.00000
41	.223144	.513551	1.00000
42	.189325	0.00000	0.00000
43	0.00000	.322222	0.00000
44	.589927E-01	.361005	0.00000
45	.181283	0.00000	0.00000
46	0.00000	.402400	1.00000
47	.487342E-01	.551579	1.00000
48	.614579	.507935	0.00000
49	.362762	.218797	0.00000
50	.465305	.238758	1.00000
51	.164191	.313050	0.00000
52	.956033E-01	.226437	1.00000
53	.113832	.910705E-01	1.00000

	OEXP80	OEXP78	DREP
54	.597434	.187584	0.00000
55	.129360	.863333E-01	1.00000
56	.395097	.549373	0.00000
57	.260439	.582904	0.00000
58	.458988	.401828	0.00000
59	.125624E-01	.214118	1.00000
60	.178609	.361217	0.00000
61	.414117	.295053	1.00000
62	.259407	.637610	0.00000
63	.396753	.341177	0.00000
64	.201753	.191868	1.00000
65	.781966	.611049	0.00000
66	.267034	.179835	0.00000
67	0.00000	0.00000	0.00000
68	.799686E-01	.945223E-01	0.00000
69	0.00000	.691058	1.00000
70	.128836E-02	0.00000	0.00000
71	.531286E-01	0.00000	0.00000
72	0.00000	.404262	0.00000
73	.172933	0.00000	1.00000
74	.431431	.590824	0.00000
75	.232927	0.00000	0.00000
76	.193001	.502352	0.00000
77	.315989	.578834	0.00000
78	.639399	0.00000	0.00000
79	0.00000	0.00000	0.00000
80	.372105	0.00000	0.00000
81	.257282	.160969	0.00000
82	.155067	.588018	1.00000
83	.222536E-01	.285842E-01	0.00000
84	.290123	0.00000	0.00000
85	0.00000	.112802	0.00000
86	.711270E-01	0.00000	0.00000
87	0.00000	.968601E-01	0.00000
88	0.00000	.324854E-01	0.00000
89	.126981	.348500	1.00000
90	0.00000	.340181	0.00000

	OEXP80	OEXP78	DREP
91	.369659	.498290	1.00000
92	.937369E-01	0.00000	0.00000
93	.172183	.427392E-01	1.00000
94	.272090	.280810	0.00000
95	0.00000	0.00000	0.00000
96	.162316	0.00000	0.00000
97	0.00000	.697561E-01	0.00000
98	.469828E-01	0.00000	1.00000
99	0.00000	.424466	1.00000
100	0.00000	0.00000	1.00000
101	0.00000	.106074	1.00000
102	.183628	.116039	1.00000
103	.244255	0.00000	1.00000
104	0.00000	0.00000	1.00000
105	.559893	.585257E-01	1.00000
106	.156934	0.00000	1.00000
107	.106480	.194528	1.00000
108	.356230	.224769	0.00000
109	.163695	.123860	0.00000
110	0.00000	.254555	0.00000
111	.160141	.146210	0.00000
112	.354134	.290168	0.00000
113	.382982	0.00000	1.00000
114	.656969	.704853	0.00000
115	.263892	.542164	1.00000
116	.382347	.327857	1.00000
117	0.00000	.303527	0.00000
118	.628782	.546195	0.00000
119	.917100	.752652	0.00000
120	.165628	.338718	1.00000
121	.296525	.361086	1.00000
122	.732547	.181203	0.00000
123	.495984	.309711	0.00000
124	.555358	.127798	0.00000
125	.321023	.304365	1.00000
126	.382132	0.00000	1.00000
127	.256809	.446484	0.00000

	OEXP80	OEXP78	DREP
128	.104769E-01	.305991	1.00000
129	0.00000	0.00000	0.00000
130	.702460	0.00000	0.00000
131	.163088	0.00000	0.00000
132	.314039	.197504	1.00000
133	.208998	.315850	1.00000
134	0.00000	0.00000	0.00000
135	0.00000	0.00000	1.00000
136	.185515	0.00000	0.00000
137	.518774	.343022	0.00000
138	0.00000	.234658	0.00000
139	.470980	0.00000	1.00000
140	0.00000	.397428	0.00000
141	.166469	.361421E-01	0.00000
142	.364340	.268948	1.00000
143	.100282	.374234	1.00000
144	.311007	.287399	1.00000
145	.622084	.332222	0.00000
146	0.00000	0.00000	0.00000
147	.589853E-01	.258318	1.00000
148	.201134	.307546	0.00000
149	.309695	0.00000	0.00000
150	0.00000	.699985E-01	0.00000
151	.617935	.547707	0.00000
152	.152913	0.00000	1.00000
153	0.00000	0.00000	0.00000
154	0.00000	.145897	0.00000
155	.252579	.350829	0.00000
156	.409251	.389240	0.00000
157	0.00000	0.00000	0.00000
158	.713652E-01	0.00000	0.00000
159	.360634	0.00000	0.00000
160	.373961	.272286	1.00000
161	0.00000	0.00000	0.00000
162	.375632	0.00000	0.00000
163	0.00000	0.00000	0.00000
164	.474814	.223093	1.00000

	OEXP80	OEXP78	DREP
165	.672675	.525284	0.00000
166	.135628	0.00000	1.00000
167	.355423	.341219	1.00000
168	.701689	.454524	0.00000
169	0.00000	.335313	0.00000
170	.220201	.296013	0.00000
171	0.00000	.135597	1.00000
172	.536448	.362733	0.00000
173	.259977	.452680	1.00000
174	.339105	.366537	0.00000
175	0.00000	0.00000	0.00000
176	.131415E-01	0.00000	0.00000
177	0.00000	0.00000	0.00000
178	0.00000	0.00000	0.00000
179	.103072	0.00000	1.00000
180	0.00000	.434090	1.00000
181	.138504	.113513	1.00000
182	0.00000	.462476	1.00000
183	.713304	.488785	0.00000
184	0.00000	.604687	0.00000
185	.486760	.369518	1.00000
186	.903085E-01	0.00000	0.00000
187	.526403	.450579	0.00000
188	.274868	.502001	0.00000
189	0.00000	0.00000	0.00000
190	0.00000	.555190	1.00000
191	.309325	0.00000	1.00000
192	0.00000	.309142	0.00000
193	.387864	.484029	0.00000
194	0.00000	0.00000	0.00000
195	.162932E-0	10.00000	0.00000
196	.913327E-01	.120737	0.00000
197	.107746	.504788	1.00000
198	0.00000	.193114	1.00000
199	.526138	0.00000	0.00000
200	.573082	0.00000	0.00000
201	.198707	.576007	0.00000

	OEXP80	OEXP78	DREP
202	.145853	.860801E-01	1.00000
203	.766113E-01	.494786	1.00000
204	.145890	.376377	1.00000
205	.130189	.144573	0.00000
206	.396819	.345103	0.00000
207	.139022	0.00000	0.00000
208	.583388	0.00000	0.00000
209	.439712	.540683	0.00000
210	.318654	.190405	0.00000
211	.180531	.413246	1.00000
212	.441106	.408532	1.00000
213	.542968	.412992	0.00000
214	.609793E-01	.800718E-01	0.00000
215	.556667	.586715	1.00000
216	0.00000	0.00000	0.00000
217	.180008	0.00000	0.00000
218	0.00000	.656993E-01	1.00000
219	.656830E-01	.372900	1.00000
220	.245520	.832426E-01	0.00000
221	.564318	.290467	1.00000
222	.380174	.370254	1.00000
223	.275748	.181455	0.00000
224	.896337	.795080	0.00000
225	.131045	.123376	1.00000
226	.816403	.660403	0.00000
227	0.00000	0.00000	0.00000
228	0.00000	0.00000	0.00000
229	.142418	.224614	0.00000
230	0.00000	0.00000	0.00000
231	0.00000	0.00000	0.00000
232	0.00000	0.00000	0.00000
233	0.00000	0.00000	0.00000
234	.411592E-02	0.00000	0.00000
235	.465941	.181086	0.00000
236	.329557	.193252	0.00000
237	.469616	.662242	1.00000
238	0.00000	0.00000	0.00000

	OEXP80	OEXP78	DREP
239	0.00000	.361805	0.00000
240	0.00000	0.00000	0.00000
241	0.00000	0.00000	0.00000
242	.383642	.572354	0.00000
243	.317159	.428523	0.00000
244	0.00000	0.00000	1.00000
245	0.00000	.120342	1.00000
246	.409744	.410363	0.00000
247	0.00000	.263538	0.00000
248	.263006	.481132	1.00000
249	.760361E-01	.471891	1.00000
250	.396714E-01	.299623	1.00000
251	0.00000	0.00000	1.00000
252	0.00000	.342477	1.00000
253	.333925	.175863	0.00000
254	0.00000	0.00000	0.00000
255	0.00000	.908178E-01	1.00000
256	.399431	.414707	0.00000
257	0.00000	0.00000	0.00000
258	.273597	.250179	0.00000
259	.235807	.231974	0.00000
260	.451499	0.00000	0.00000
261	.400779	.415548	0.00000
262	.584520	.362387	0.00000
263	.205794	.453670	0.00000
264	.189447	.235386	0.00000
265	.174426	.129949	1.00000
266	.702078E-01	0.00000	1.00000
267	.664887	.285268	0.00000
268	0.00000	.130419	1.00000
269	.292894	.544172	0.00000
270	.388511	.615662	0.00000
271	.103930	0.00000	1.00000
272	.236982	.468540	1.00000
273	.285047E-01	.312937	1.00000
274	0.00000	0.00000	1.00000
275	.599545	.271333	0.00000

	OEXP80	OEXP78	DREP
276	.191113	.337039	1.00000
277	.329143	0.00000	1.00000
278	.575867	.550082	1.00000
279	.109582	.644687	0.00000
280	.616494	.376700	0.00000
281	0.00000	.570553E-01	1.00000
282	.203981	0.00000	1.00000
283	.111093E-01	0.00000	1.00000
284	.350524	.477296	0.00000
285	.481439	.623618	1.00000
286	0.00000	0.00000	0.00000
287	0.00000	.361546	0.00000
288	0.00000	.216046	0.00000
289	.390427	.529435	0.00000
290	.432087	.407168	0.00000
291	0.00000	0.00000	0.00000
292	.143781	.222791E-01	1.00000
293	0.00000	.372325	0.00000
294	.165648	.557493	0.00000
295	.497391	0.00000	0.00000
296	.612875	.535874	0.00000
297	0.00000	.992048E-01	0.00000
298	.175258	.605477E-01	0.00000
299	.492079	.549988	1.00000
300	.343541E-01	.412659E-01	1.00000
301	.166168	0.00000	0.00000
302	.461632	.603335	0.00000
303	.654876	.286415	0.00000
304	0.00000	.103042	1.00000
305	0.00000	0.00000	1.00000
306	.117100	.312551	0.00000
307	.204116	.234223	1.00000
308	.393401	.674553	1.00000
309	0.00000	0.00000	1.00000
310	.500334	.480844	0.00000
311	.440400	.522478	0.00000
312	.217154	0.00000	1.00000

	OEXP80	OEXP78	DREP
313	.162312E-01	0.00000	0.00000
314	0.00000	.474909	0.00000
315	.633181E-02	0.00000	0.00000
316	0.00000	.410519	1.00000
317	.453949	.170249	1.00000
318	.635810	.461512	0.00000
319	0.00000	.439642	0.00000
320	.633748	.388830	0.00000
321	.209262	.282028	1.00000
322	.428037	.428058	0.00000
323	0.00000	0.00000	1.00000
324	.672133E-03	.568253	0.00000
325	.616205	0.00000	0.00000
326	.291059	0.00000	0.00000
327	0.00000	.174765	1.00000
328	.258059	0.00000	1.00000
329	.213326	0.00000	0.00000
330	.157092	0.00000	0.00000
331	.467591	.175064	0.00000
332	0.00000	.610818E-01	1.00000
333	0.00000	.285677	0.00000
334	0.00000	.645666E-01	0.00000
335	0.00000	.633711	0.00000
336	.232132E-01	.313772E-01	0.00000
337	0.00000	0.00000	1.00000
338	.333649	.483718	0.00000
339	0.00000	.194898	0.00000
340	.301632E-01	0.00000	1.00000
341	.634627	.327826	0.00000
342	0.00000	0.00000	0.00000
343	.200871	.291912	0.00000
344	0.00000	.352292	0.00000
345	.339370	.425133E-01	0.00000
346	.318374	.403098	0.00000
347	.210081	.263872	0.00000
348	0.00000	.244167	0.00000
349	0.00000	.311094	0.00000

	OEXP80	OEXP78	DREP
350	0.00000	0.00000	0.00000
351	0.00000	.580638	0.00000
352	.250674	0.00000	0.00000
353	.116489	.521250	1.00000
354	.676189	.596805	1.00000
355	.260962E-01	.873901E-01	0.00000
356	.236931	.397175	0.00000
357	.457532	.497326	0.00000
358	.727932E-01	.394948	1.00000
359	0.00000	.116353	1.00000
360	0.00000	.342572	1.00000
361	0.00000	0.00000	1.00000
362	.311005	0.00000	1.00000
363	0.00000	0.00000	0.00000
364	0.00000	0.00000	1.00000
365	0.00000	.401793	1.00000
366	.632218	.576767	0.00000
367	.161007	.333781	1.00000
368	.629599	.611881	0.00000
369	.350109	.324067	1.00000
370	.949539E-01	.683222	0.00000
371	.254848	.544327	0.00000
372	.616396	.330890	0.00000
373	.371862	.334853	0.00000
374	.413346	.103785	0.00000
375	.483469	.709404	0.00000
376	.512548	.272713	0.00000
377	0.00000	0.00000	0.00000
378	.332118	.581454	0.00000
379	.555744	.663467	0.00000
380	.566001	.665135E-01	0.00000
381	.411447	.585125	0.00000
382	.296330E-01	.677948E-01	0.00000
383	.224322	.200446	0.00000
384	.123087	.263297	1.00000
385	.183171E-01	.171826	1.00000
386	0.00000	.456074	1.00000

The data listed below are for the U.S. Senate and are used in Chapter 6. Each pair are one state and are in alphabetical order from Alabama to Wyoming. Within each state, the senators are arranged by the list of senators given in the *Congressional Quarterly* roll call votes for 1977. The following senator (and corresponding observations) did not vote: Heflin (2), DeConcini (6), Pryor (8), Hart (12), Hawkins (17), Inouye (21), Percy (25), Dixon (26), Grassley (29), Jepsen (30), Huddleston (34), Cohen (37), Sarbanes(40), Boshwitz (45), Baucus (51), Nickles (71), Boren (72), Tower (85), and Evans (93).

	VOTE	DED	DDEM
1	1.00000	75.6000	0.00000
2	0.00000	75.6000	1.00000
3	0.00000	57.8000	1.00000
4	1.00000	57.8000	1.00000
5	0.00000	65.2000	0.00000
6	0.00000	65.2000	1.00000
7	0.00000	78.4000	1.00000
8	0.00000	78.4000	1.00000
9	1.00000	60.8000	0.00000
10	0.00000	60.8000	1.00000
11	1.00000	54.0000	0.00000
12	0.00000	54.0000	1.00000
13	1.00000	58.6000	0.00000
14	0.00000	58.6000	1.00000
15	1.00000	65.0000	0.00000
16	0.00000	65.0000	0.00000
17	0.00000	70.2000	0.00000
18	0.00000	70.2000	1.00000
19	0.00000	70.8000	0.00000
20	0.00000	70.8000	1.00000
21	0.00000	59.4000	1.00000
22	0.00000	59.4000	1.00000
23	1.00000	68.4000	0.00000
24	1.00000	68.4000	1.00000
25	0.00000	67.6000	0.00000
26	0.00000	67.6000	1.00000
27	1.00000	75.0000	0.00000

	VOTE	DED	DDEM
28	1.00000	75.0000	0.00000
29	0.00000	72.2000	0.00000
30	0.00000	72.2000	0.00000
31	0.00000	66.0000	0.00000
32	1.00000	66.0000	0.00000
33	0.00000	77.8000	1.00000
34	0.00000	77.8000	1.00000
35	0.00000	72.2000	1.00000
36	0.00000	72.2000	1.00000
37	0.00000	71.2000	0.00000
38	1.00000	71.2000	1.00000
39	1.00000	59.2000	0.00000
40	0.00000	59.2000	1.00000
41	0.00000	60.0000	1.00000
42	0.00000	60.0000	1.00000
43	0.00000	71.4000	1.00000
44	0.00000	71.4000	1.00000
45	0.00000	65.2000	0.00000
46	0.00000	65.2000	0.00000
47	1.00000	75.4000	0.00000
48	0.00000	75.4000	1.00000
49	0.00000	72.2000	0.00000
50	0.00000	72.2000	1.00000
51	0.00000	65.0000	1.00000
52	0.00000	65.0000	1.00000
53	1.00000	69.0000	1.00000
54	1.00000	69.0000	1.00000
55	0.00000	71.2000	0.00000
56	0.00000	71.2000	0.00000
57	1.00000	63.6000	0.00000
58	1.00000	63.6000	0.00000
59	0.00000	63.4000	1.00000
60	0.00000	63.4000	1.00000
61	0.00000	64.8000	0.00000
62	0.00000	64.8000	1.00000
63	0.00000	64.2000	0.00000
64	1.00000	64.2000	1.00000

	VOTE	DED	DDEM
65	0.00000	73.6000	0.00000
66	0.00000	73.6000	0.00000
67	1.00000	70.4000	0.00000
68	0.00000	70.4000	1.00000
69	0.00000	72.6000	1.00000
70	1.00000	72.6000	1.00000
71	0.00000	69.8000	0.00000
72	0.00000	69.8000	1.00000
73	0.00000	64.2000	0.00000
74	1.00000	64.2000	0.00000
75	1.00000	72.8000	0.00000
76	1.00000	72.8000	0.00000
77	1.00000	69.2000	0.00000
78	1.00000	69.2000	1.00000
79	1.00000	73.2000	0.00000
80	0.00000	73.2000	1.00000
81	1.00000	72.0000	0.00000
82	1.00000	72.0000	0.00000
83	1.00000	74.8000	0.00000
84	0.00000	74.8000	1.00000
85	0.00000	66.2000	0.00000
86	0.00000	66.2000	1.00000
87	1.00000	60.2000	0.00000
88	1.00000	60.2000	0.00000
89	0.00000	62.0000	0.00000
90	0.00000	62.0000	1.00000
91	1.00000	61.8000	0.00000
92	1.00000	61.8000	0.00000
93	0.00000	62.0000	0.00000
94	1.00000	62.0000	0.00000
95	0.00000	79.2000	1.00000
96	0.00000	79.2000	1.00000
97	1.00000	70.4000	0.00000
98	0.00000	70.4000	1.00000
99	0.00000	65.6000	0.00000
100	1.00000	65.6000	0.00000

	TENURE	LVOTE	D86
1	4.00000	50.0000	1.00000
2	6.00000	94.0000	0.00000
3	4.00000	54.0000	1.00000
4	16.0000	76.0000	0.00000
5	16.0000	50.0000	1.00000
6	8.00000	59.0000	0.00000
7	10.0000	59.0000	1.00000
8	6.00000	77.0000	0.00000
9	2.00000	52.0000	0.00000
10	16.0000	57.0000	1.00000
11	6.00000	59.0000	0.00000
12	10.0000	50.0000	1.00000
13	14.0000	50.0000	0.00000
14	4.00000	56.0000	1.00000
15	14.0000	56.0000	0.00000
16	12.0000	58.0000	0.00000
17	4.00000	52.0000	1.00000
18	14.0000	62.0000	0.00000
19	4.00000	51.0000	1.00000
20	12.0000	83.0000	0.00000
21	22.0000	78.0000	1.00000
22	8.00000	80.0000	0.00000
23	12.0000	68.0000	0.00000
24	4.00000	50.0000	1.00000
25	18.0000	53.0000	0.00000
26	4.00000	56.0000	1.00000
27	8.00000	54.0000	0.00000
28	4.00000	54.0000	1.00000
29	4.00000	53.0000	1.00000
30	6.00000	51.0000	0.00000
31	16.0000	64.0000	1.00000
32	6.00000	54.0000	0.00000
33	10.0000	65.0000	1.00000
34	12.0000	61.0000	0.00000
35	12.0000	59.0000	0.00000
36	36.0000	58.0000	1.00000
37	6.00000	57.0000	0.00000

	TENURE	LVOTE	D86
38	4.00000	61.0000	0.00000
39	16.0000	66.0000	1.00000
40	8.00000	63.0000	0.00000
41	22.0000	61.0000	0.00000
42	6.00000	55.0000	0.00000
43	6.00000	52.0000	0.00000
44	8.00000	58.0000	0.00000
45	6.00000	57.0000	0.00000
46	6.00000	53.0000	0.00000
47	6.00000	45.0000	0.00000
48	37.0000	64.0000	0.00000
49	8.00000	51.0000	0.00000
50	16.0000	52.0000	1.00000
51	6.00000	56.0000	0.00000
52	8.00000	54.0000	0.00000
53	6.00000	68.0000	0.00000
54	8.00000	67.0000	0.00000
55	2.00000	50.0000	0.00000
56	10.0000	59.0000	1.00000
57	6.00000	51.0000	0.00000
58	4.00000	52.0000	0.00000
59	6.00000	56.0000	0.00000
60	2.00000	51.0000	0.00000
61	12.0000	53.0000	0.00000
62	2.00000	54.0000	0.00000
63	4.00000	45.0000	1.00000
64	8.00000	65.0000	0.00000
65	4.00000	50.0000	1.00000
66	12.0000	55.0000	0.00000
67	4.00000	70.0000	1.00000
68	24.0000	62.0000	0.00000
69	10.0000	69.0000	1.00000
70	8.00000	57.0000	0.00000
71	4.00000	53.0000	1.00000
72	6.00000	65.0000	0.00000
73	18.0000	62.0000	0.00000
74	16.0000	52.0000	1.00000

	TENURE	LVOTE	D86
75	8.00000	59.0000	0.00000
76	4.00000	50.0000	1.00000
77	8.00000	51.0000	0.00000
78	24.0000	75.0000	0.00000
79	28.0000	56.0000	0.00000
80	18.0000	70.0000	1.00000
81	4.00000	58.0000	1.00000
82	6.00000	67.0000	0.00000
83	18.0000	56.0000	0.00000
84	8.00000	62.0000	0.00000
85	23.0000	50.0000	0.00000
86	14.0000	59.0000	0.00000
87	10.0000	74.0000	1.00000
88	26.0000	58.0000	0.00000
89	13.0000	51.0000	0.00000
90	10.0000	50.0000	1.00000
91	2.00000	51.0000	0.00000
92	6.00000	50.0000	0.00000
93	0.00000	0.00000	0.00000
94	4.00000	54.0000	1.00000
95	26.0000	69.0000	0.00000
96	26.0000	50.0000	0.00000
97	4.00000	50.0000	1.00000
98	27.0000	64.0000	0.00000
99	6.00000	62.0000	0.00000
100	8.00000	57.0000	0.00000

BIBLIOGRAPHY

Abrams, B. H. and Settle, R. F., "The Effect of Broadcasting on Political Campaign Spending: An Empirical Investigation." *Journal of Political Economy,* 84 (October 1976), pp. 1095-1108.

Adams, J. D. and Kenny, L. W., "Optimal Tenure of Elected Officials." *Journal of Law and Economics,* XXIX (2) October 1986, pp. 303-328.

Akerlof, G.A., "The Market for 'Lemons': Qualitative Uncertainty and the Market Mechanism." *Quarterly Journal of Economics,* 84 (August 1970), pp. 488-500.

Ashenfelter, O. and Kelley S. Jr., "Determinants of Participation in Presidential Elections." *Journal of Law and Economics,* 18 (December 1975), pp. 695-733.

Barone, M. and Ujifusa, G., *Almanac of American Politics.* (Washington, D.C.: National Journal, 1983).

Barzel, Y. and Silberberg, E., "Is the Act of Voting Rational?" *Public Choice,* 16 (Fall 1973), pp. 51-58.

Blakely, S., "Prospects Seen Brightening for Senate TV." *Congressional Quarterly Weekly,* 43 (September 21, 1985), pp. 1877-1878.

Bonafede, D., "On Television." *National Journal,* 17 (October 5, 1985), p. 2288.

Buchanan, J. M. and Tullock, G., *Calculus of Consent.* (Ann Arbor: University of Michigan Press, 1962).

Cohen, R. E., "Wide-Angle Coverage." *National Journal,* 16 (May 19, 1984), p. 997.

Cohen, R. E., "The Congress Watchers." *National Journal,* 17 (January 26, 1985), p. 215.

Cohen, R. E., "C-SPAN Junkies," *National Journal.*

Congressional Quarterly, *Congressional Districts in the 1970's.* (Washington, D.C.: Congressional Quarterly, 1974).

Congressional Quarterly, *Congressional Districts in the 1980's.* (Washington, D.C.: Congressional Quarterly, 1983).

Cooper, A., "No Sideline Shots: House Gets Set to Televise Sessions with its Own Hand on the Camera." *Congressional Quarterly Weekly Report,* 35 (December 17, 1977), pp. 2605-2608.

Cooper, A., "Hollywood on the Hill: Curtain Rising on House TV Amid Aid-to-Incumbent Fears." *Congressional Quarterly Weekly Report,* 37 (February 10, 1979), pp. 252-256.

Council of State Governments, *The Book of the States, 1976-1977.* (Lexington, Kentucky: Iron Works Pike, 1976).

Council of State Governments, *The Book of the States, 1978-1979.* (Lexington, Kentucky: Iron Works Pike, 1978).

Crain, W. M., "On the Structure and Stability of Political Markets." *Journal of Political Economy,* 85 (August 1977), pp. 829-842.

Crain, W. M., "Attenuated Property Rights and the Market for Governors." *Journal of Law and Economics,* 1977.

Crain, W. M., "Cost and Output in the Legislative Firm." *Journal of Legal Studies,* 8 (June 1979), pp. 607-622.

Crain, W. M., "The Sizes of Majorities." *Southern Economic Journal,* 46 (January 1980), pp. 726-734.

Crain, W. M., Leavens, D. R., and Abbot, L., "Voting and Not Voting at the Same Time." *Public Choice,* (March 1987).

Crain, W. M., Leavens, D. R. and Tollison, R. D., "Final Voting in a Legislature." *American Economic Review,* (September 1986) pp. 833-841.

Crain, W. M., and Tollison, R. D., "Campaign Expenditures and Political Competition." *Journal of Law and Economics,* 19 (April 1976), pp. 177-188.

Darby, M. R. and Karni, E., "Free Competition and the Optimal Amount of Fraud." *Journal of Law and Economics,* 16 (April 1973), pp. 67-88.

Dougan, W. R. and Munger, M. C., "The Rationality of Ideology." Unpublished manuscript, 1986.

Downs, A., *An Economic Theory of Democracy.* (New York: Harpers and Row, 1957).

Faith, R. L. and Tollison, R. D., "Voter Search for Efficient Representation." *Research in Law and Economics,* 5 (1983), pp. 211-224.

Federal Election Commision, *FEC Reports on Financial Activity 1977-1978: U.S. House and Senate Campaigns. (Washington, D.C.: Federal Election Commission, 1979).*

Ferguson, J. M., "Comment." *Journal of Law and Economics,* 29 (August 1976), pp. 341-346.

Frey, B., "Why Do High Income People Participate More in Politics?" *Public Choice,* 11 (Fall 1971), pp. 101-105.

Garay, R. G., "Factors Related to Congressional Television Implementation: A Legislative History of Television Coverage of U.S. House and Senate Committee Hearings, Meetings, and Deliberative Chamber." Ph.D. Dissertation, Ohio University, 1980.

Granat, D., "Televised Partisan Skirmishes Erupt in House." *Congressional Quarterly Weekly,* 42 (February 11, 1984), pp. 246-249.

Granat, D., "Political Uses of House Tapes Generating Inter-Party Static." *Congressional Quarterly Weekly,* 42 (May 12, 1984), p. 1129.

Granat, D., "The House's TV War: The Gloves Come Out." *Congressional Quarterly Weekly,* 42 (May 19, 1984), pp. 1166-1167.

Heard, A. ed., *State Legislatures in American Politics.* (Englewood Cliffs, N.J.: Prentice-Hall, 1966).

Jacobson, G. C., "The Effects of Campaign Spending in Congressional Elections." *American Political Science Review,* 72 (June 1978), pp. 469-491.

Jacobson, G. C., *Money in Congressional Elections.* (New Haven: Yale University Press, 1980).

Johnsen, T. H., "Advertising, Market Equilibrium, and Information." Ph.D. Dissertation, Carnegie-Mellon University, 1976.

Kalt, J. P., "The Apparent Ideological Behavior of Legislators: Testing for Principal-Agent Slack in Political Institutions." Harvard University Working Paper, 1985.

Kau, J. B. and Rubin, P. H., "Self-Interest, Ideology, and Logrolling in Congressional Voting." *Journal of Law and Economics,* 22 (October 1979), pp. 365-385.

Kihlstrom, R. E. and Riordan, M. H., "Advertising as a Signal." *Journal of Political Economy,* 92 (June 1984), pp. 427-450.

Klein, B., Crawford, R. G. and Alchain, A. A., "Vertical Integration, Appropriable Rents, and the Competetive Contracting Process." *Journal of Law and Economics,* 21 (October 1978), pp. 297-326.

Klein, B. and Leffler, K. B., "The Role of Market Forces in Assuring Contractual Performance." *Journal of Political Economy,* 89 (August 1981), pp. 615-641.

Leavens, D. R., "Legislative Compensation and the Determinants of Committee Action in the U.S. House of Representatives." Ph.D. Dissertation, George Mason University, 1984.

Lott, J. R., "Brand Names and Barriers to Entry in Political Markets." *Public Choice,* 51 (Spring 1986), pp. 87-92.

Lott, J. R., "Political Cheating." Unpublished manuscript, Texas A&M University, 1986.

Lott, J. R., "Televising Legislatures: A Note on Whether Politicans are Search Goods." Unpublished manuscript, Hoover Institution, 1986.

McCormick, R. E. and Tollison, R. D., "Legislatures as Unions." *Journal of Political Economy,* 86 (February 1978), pp. 63-78.

McCormick, R. E. and Tollison, R. D., *Politicians, Legislation, and the Economy.* (Boston: Martinus Nijhoff, 1981).

Miller, J. C., III, "A Program for Direct and Proxy Voting in the Legislative Process." *Public Choice,* Fall 1969, pp. 107-113.

Mueller, D. C., *Public Choice.* (Cambridge: Cambridge University Press, 1979).

Nelson, P., "Information and Consumer Behavior." *Journal of Political Economy,* 78 (March/April 1970), pp. 311-329.

Nelson, P., "Advertising as Information." *Journal of Political Economy,* 82 (July/August 1974), pp. 729-754.

Nelson, P., "Political Information." *Journal of Law and Economics,* 29 (August 1976), pp. 315-336.

Olson, M., *The Logic of Collective Action.* (Cambridge: Harvard University Press, 1965).

Palda, K., "The Effects of Expenditures on Election Outcomes." *Journal of Law and Economics,* 18 (December 1975), pp. 745-772.

Peabody, R., Ornstein, N. and Rhode D., "The United States Senate as a Presidential Incubator: Many are Called but Few are Chosen." *Political Science Quarterly,* 91 (Summer 1976), pp. 237-258.

Peltzman, S., "Toward a More General Theory of Regulation." *Journal of Law and Economics,* 19 (August 1976), pp. 211-240.

Randolph, E., "Network News Confronts Era of Limits." *The Washington Post,* February 9, 1987, p. A4.

Riker, W. H., *The Theory of Political Coalitions.* (New Haven: Yale University Press, 1962).

Riker, W. and Ordeshook, P. C., "A Theory of the Calculus of Voting." *American Political Science Review,* 62 (March 1968), pp. 25-42.

Roberts, S. V., "T.V. May Quicken the Senate's Pluse," *The New York Times,* June 8, 1986, p. E5.

Robinson, M. J. and Appel, K. R., "Network News Coverage of Congress." *Political Science Quarterly,* 94 (Fall 1979), pp. 407-418.

Rundquist, P. S. and Nickels, I. B., "Senate Television: Its Impact on Senate Floor Proceedings." Congressional Research Service, 1986.

Russell, K. P., Fraser, J. and Frey, B.S., "Political Participation and Income Level: An Exchange." *Public Choice,* 13 (Fall 1972), pp. 113-122.

Scammon, R. M. and McGilivray, A. V. eds., *America Votes 14.* (Washington,

D.C.: Congressional Quarterly, 1981).

Schmalensee, R., "A Model of Advertising and Product Quality." *Journal of Political Economy,* 86 (June 1978), pp. 485-503.

Schmalensee, R., "Product Differentiation Advantages of Pioneering Brands." *American Economic Review,* 72 (June 1982), pp. 349-365.

Sisk, B. F., "Address in U.S. House of Representatives." *Congressional Record* (October 27, 1977), pp. 35426-35430.

Spence, M. A., "Job Market Signaling." *Quarterly Journal of Economics,* 87 (August 1973), pp. 355-374.

Spence, M. A., "Notes on Advertising, Economics of Scale, and Entry Barriers." *Quarterly Journal of Economics,* 95 (November, 1980), pp. 493-504.

Stevens, A. G., "Televising Floor Proceedings in State Legislatures: A Summary of Survey Findings." In *Senate Communications with the Public.* (94th Congress, 2nd Session, 1977).

Stigler, G. J., "The Economics of Information." *Journal of Political Economy,* 69 (June 1961), pp. 213-225.

Stigler, G. J., "The Sizes of Legislatures." *Journal of Legal Studies,* 17 (January 1976), pp. 17-34.

Telser, L. G., "Comment." *Journal of Law and Economics,* 29 (August 1976), pp. 337-340.

Telser, L. G., "A Theory of Self-Enforcing Agreements." *Journal of Business,* 22 (January 1980), pp. 27-44.

Thomas, S. J., "Does Incumbent Campaign Spending Matter?" Unpublished manuscript, University of California, Irvine, 1986.

Tollison, R. D., Crain, W. M. and Pautler, P., "Information and Voting: An Empirical Note." *Public Choice,* 26 (Winter 1975), pp. 43-49.

Tollison, R. D. and Willett, T. D., "Some Simple Economics of Voting and Not Voting." *Public Choice,* 24 (Fall 1973), pp. 59-72.

Tullock, G., "Entry Barriers into Politics." *American Economic Review,* 55 (May 1967), pp. 458-466.

Tullock, G., *Toward a Mathematics of Politics.* (Ann Arbor: University of Michigan Press, 1967).

U.S. Bureau of the Census, *Statistical Abstract of the United States: 1985.* (Washington, D.C.: U.S. Government Printing Office, 1984).

U.S. Congress Advisory Commission on Intergovernmental Relations, *Apportionment of State Legislatures.* (Washington, D.C.: U.S. Government Printing Office, 1962).

Uston, K., "Senate Report Cards." The Uston Institute, San Francisco, 1986.

Welch, W. P., "The Economics of Campaign Funds." *Public Choice,* 20 (Winter 1974), pp. 83-97.

Welch, W. P., "The Effectiveness of Expenditures on State Legislative Races." *American Politics Quarterly,* 4 (July 1976), pp. 333-356.

Welch, W. P., "Money and Votes: A Simultaneous Equation Model." *Public Choice,* 36 (Number 2 1981), pp. 209-232.

INDEX